ACTION 2000

Praying Scripture
in a Contemporaray Way

Mark Link, S.J.

C
Cycle

PUBLISHING
Allen, Texas

IMPRIMI POTEST
Bradley M. Schaeffer, S.J.

NIHIL OBSTAT
Rev. Glenn D. Gardner, J.C.D.
Censor Liborum

IMPRIMATUR
† Most Rev. Charles V. Grahmann
Bishop of Dallas

October 10, 1993

The *Nihil Obstat* and *Imprimatur* are official declarations
that the work contains nothing contrary to Faith and
Morals. It is not implied thereby that those granting the
Nihil Obstat and *Imprimatur* agree with the contents,
statements, or opinions expressed.

ACKNOWLEDGMENT

Unless otherwise noted, Scripture quotations are from
Today's English Version text. Copyright © American
Bible Society 1966, 1971, 1976. Used by permission.

Send all inquiries to:
Tabor Publishing
200 East Bethany Drive
Allen, Texas 75002–3804

Printed in Korea

ISBN 0-7829-0362-2

   2 3 4 5   98 97 96 95 94

Books in the Vision 2000 Program

The following books in the Vision 2000 Program are available or projected for future publication:

Vision 2000 (A Cycle)
Mission 2000 (B Cycle)
Action 2000 (C Cycle)
Challenge 2000
Bible 2000
Almanac 2000

Quantity discounts are available when ordering multiple copies. For further information on these books or discount offers, call or write:

Tabor Publishing
200 East Bethany Drive
Allen, Texas 75002-3804
Call toll free 800-822-6701

VISION 2000

is a daily
meditation program.

Action 2000, the third book
of the Vision 2000 Program,
is based on the common Lectionary
readings for—

Sunday: Gospel (C Cycle)
Weekday: Reading I, Year I

For other books in the program,
see opposite inside front cover.

CONTENTS

CONTENTS

About *Action 2000*

Action 2000 is the third book of the Vision 2000 Program.

The Vision 2000 Program was inspired by the fall of the Berlin Wall. Something nobody thought could happen in a hundred years happened in a hundred days.

If this history-making event could happen so quickly, against such incredible odds, is it not a "sign" that other "walls" can fall just as quickly against equally incredible odds:

- walls of prejudice,
- walls of injustice,
- walls of ignorance,
- walls of hatred?

Many people believe that it is.

The Vision 2000 Program is an invitation for these people to join hands and to pray for an outpouring of the Holy Spirit on our world as it crosses the threshold into the new century.

It is an invitation to pray that the twenty-first century will witness a new "fall of walls" that will lead to a new union and solidarity of the human family.

How to Use *Action 2000*

Like the first two books of this program
(*Vision 2000* and *Mission 2000*), *Action 2000*
is based on the common Lectionary readings.
That is, it follows the Sunday and daily
Scripture readings used in public worship
by Catholics and many Protestants.

There are two ways to use this book:

— on your own or
— as a member of a support group.

If you pray it *on your own,* simply devote ten
minutes a day to the daily meditation exercise.

If you pray it *as a member of a support group,*
spend ten minutes a day on the daily meditation
exercise and then meet with five to seven other
people once a week. This is the ideal way to
use this book.

Guidelines for Daily Meditation

Each meditation exercise in *Action 2000* contains the same four elements:

— a Bible reading,
— a story,
— an application to life,
— a concluding thought.

The procedure for praying each exercise is described on the inside front cover of this book. It involves four steps, or phases—read, think, speak, listen.

Perhaps the best way to understand the four phases of the meditation process is to think of the human person as having four levels:

— a *skin* or sense level,
— a *mind* or conscious level,
— a *heart* or subconscious level,
— a *soul* or sanctuary level.

The *skin* level is the level at which we experience sense contact. We see, hear, and touch one another.

The *mind* level is the level at which we experience conscious thought processes.

The *heart* level is the level at which we experience subconscious movements of the heart or spirit. For example, we may say, "I can't explain why, but I feel a deep inner peace." In other words, something in our heart level is moving us to feel this way.

The *soul* level is the level at which we experience ultimate reality. Jesus talked about it when he said, "The Kingdom of God is within you" (LUKE 17:21). Saint Paul also talked about it when he said, "The Holy Spirit . . . lives in you" (1 CORINTHIANS 6:19).

Each of these levels—sense, mind, heart, and soul—comes into play in the prayer process:

— the *sense* level, in the *reading* phase;
— the *mind* level, in the *thinking* phase;
— the *heart* level, in the *speaking* phase;
— the *soul* level, in the *listening* phase.

People sometimes ask, "How much time should I spend on each phase?"

A tentative suggestion is given in the inside front cover of the book. As we advance in prayer, however, we will develop our own time schedule. For example, we may spend more time on the fourth phase (listening) and less time on the second phase (thinking).

Guidelines for the Weekly Meetings

As noted earlier, the ideal way to use *Action 2000* is as a member of a support group that meets weekly. The purpose of the meetings is—

- to support one another in the commitment to meditate daily and
- to share with the group the experience of the daily meditations.

Specifically, it is to share with other group members—

- which meditations struck each group member the most that week and
- what thoughts or insights came to each member during those meditations.

(N.B.: Group members are encouraged to keep a prayer journal in which they make brief notation after each meditation.)

Leadership of the group is best rotated from one member to another and from one meeting to the next. Basically, the function of the leader is to open the meeting, begin the sharing session, and close the meeting.

The procedures for opening and closing all meetings ("Call to Prayer" and "Call to Mission") are described on the inside back page and the inside back cover of this book.

The leader calls each meeting to order promptly at the designated time. (Meetings are thirty to forty minutes long, unless the group decides otherwise.)

The meeting itself begins with the leader responding briefly (two minutes) to these two questions:

- How faithful was I to my commitment to meditate daily? (This question may be omitted after the members get the habit of prayer.)
- Which of the daily meditation exercises did I find especially profitable—and why?

The leader then invites each member, in turn, to respond briefly (two minutes per person) to the same two questions.

When all have responded, the leader opens the floor to anyone who wishes—

- to elaborate on his or her response to the second question or
- to comment on another's response (but not to take issue with it or to offer advice). For example, a member might say to another member, "I really was moved by what you shared. Could you elaborate on it a bit more?"

Two points are in order here.

First, the group should be patient with the sharing process. It may take a little time to develop—depending on how well the members know, trust, and bond with one another.

Second, some members may be a bit reluctant, at first, to "share their faith" with others. They will have to be gentle with themselves and with one another on this point. It takes a little time to develop. Members will find that when they begin to share, the experience is both enriching and affirming.

About the Lectionary Readings

The Lectionary readings vary from year to year, depending on the date of Easter. This leads to complications.

For simplicity's sake, therefore, brief sections of *Action 2000* are adapted. Similarly, special Lectionary readings for special days (feast days of saints) are omitted.

The Lectionary readings in this volume are based on the readings for—

- Sunday: Gospel (C Cycle)
- Weekday: Reading I, Year I

NOTE: Because the two daily readings for Advent, Christmas, Epiphany, Lent, and Easter are always the same, we have chosen the gospel reading for use in those sections of *Action 2000* (C Cycle) rather than repeat the first reading, which was used in *Mission 2000* (B Cycle).

SEASON
OF
ADVENT

[Jesus said,]
"Be careful. . . . Be on watch and pray."
LUKE 21:34, 36

Farmers hope for lots of rain
right after they plant their corn.
Once it sprouts and gets a good start,
they hope for a "dry period."
The reason is to force the corn's roots
to grow downward in search of water,
rather than stay on the surface.
Unless the tap root of the corn
grows downward to the "water level,"
the corn will wither and dry when
the heat of summer sets in—
it will have no way to draw up water.
Our prayer life is like that.
God usually gives us a good start.
Then God lets a "dry period" set in
to force our prayer roots
to grow downward to the *faith* level,
rather than stay on the surface
at the *feeling* level.

Why must prayer be primarily an exercise
of faith rather than feeling?

Pure love and prayer are learned in the
hour when prayer has become impossible
and your heart has turned to stone.
THOMAS MERTON

MONDAY
Advent
Week 1 ⎯⎯⎯⎯⎯⎯⎯⎯⎯⎯⎯

[A Roman officer said to Jesus,]
"My servant is sick in bed at home,
unable to move and suffering. . . .
Give the order,
and my servant will get well. . . ."
The officer's servant
was healed that very moment.

MATTHEW 8:6, 8, 13

A boy in Italy had been working hard
to make enough money
to continue his singing lessons.
One day his voice teacher told him
he was wasting his money—and time.
The boy's mother, a poor peasant woman,
encouraged her son to pursue his dream
in spite of the rebuff.
She even went barefoot to help him
with the money for his lessons.
Her faith and perseverance paid off;
her son, Enrico Caruso, grew up to be
one of the world's greatest tenors.

How willing am I to serve or sacrifice
for people who need me—people
like Enrico or the officer's servant?

The measure of greatness
is not the number of servants you have,
but the number of people you serve.

ANONYMOUS

[Jesus said to his disciples,]
"Many prophets and kings
wanted to see what you see,
but they could not,
and to hear what you hear,
but they did not."

LUKE 10:24

Lutheran pastor Dietrich Bonhoeffer
was imprisoned by the Nazis.
Just before Christmas 1943, he wrote:
"Life in a prison
reminds me a great deal of Advent.
One waits and hopes and putters around.
But in the end
what we do is of little consequence.
The door is shut, and
it can only be opened from the outside."
That describes
the human race before Jesus' coming.
We were imprisoned by sin.
The door was shut and couldn't be opened,
except from the outside.
That's what Jesus did; he opened the door.

What am I doing with the new freedom
Jesus won for the human race—and me?

One never notices what has been done;
one can only see what remains to be done.
MARIE CURIE

Crowds came to [Jesus], bringing with them the lame, the blind, the crippled, the dumb, and many other sick people , . . . and he healed them.

MATTHEW 15:30

Columnist Ann Landers
has been giving advice to people
for over 30 years.
One day an interviewer asked her,
"What question are you asked most?"
Ann said it was a very simple question,
"What's the matter with me?
Why am I so lonely?"
When asked what answer she gives
to this question, Ann said,
"Get involved!
Do something for other people.
And the people who need help
are all about you.
Everywhere you look, you see them."

The advice of Ann Landers
and the example of Jesus in the gospel
invite me to ask,
Who is one person whom I could help?

*Self-sacrifice
is never entirely unselfish,
for the giver never fails to receive.*

DELORES McGUIRE

[Jesus said,]
"Not everyone who calls me 'Lord, Lord'
will enter the Kingdom of heaven,
but only those who do what
my Father in heaven wants them to do."

MATTHEW 7.21

Barbara Arnstein says she got a call
from a cabdriver who told her
that she had left her purse in his taxi.
When she picked it up—with nothing
missing from it—she was so delighted
that she offered him a reward.
He refused, saying,
"Just let me know how much money
you had in your purse."
Somewhat puzzled, she told him.
He pulled out a tiny notebook
and recorded the amount, saying,
"I'm keeping tab on how much
it's costing me to be honest."

The cabdriver does
what Jesus says we must do.
We must do more
than simply pay lip service to God.
We must do what God wants us to do.
How much is my honesty costing me?

Honesty pays,
but not enough to suit some people.

FRIDAY
Advent
Week 1 _____

[Two blind men
asked Jesus to have mercy on them.
Jesus] asked them,
"Do you believe that I can heal you?"
"Yes sir!" they answered.
Then Jesus touched their eyes and said,
"Let it happen, then, just as you believe!"

MATTHEW 9:28-29

Belief in Jesus is basically
a commitment to accept Jesus
for what he claimed to be: the Son of God.
"Until one is committed,
there is hesitancy," says W. H. Murray.
"The moment
one definitely commits oneself,
then Providence moves too.
All sorts of things occur . . .
which no man could have dreamt
would have come his way."

To what extent have I committed myself
irrevocably to Jesus Christ?
Can I put my finger on one thing
"which no man could have dreamt"
that can be traced
to my commitment to Jesus Christ?

It is love that makes faith,
not faith love.

JOHN HENRY NEWMAN

Jesus said to his disciples,
"The harvest is large, but
there are few workers to gather it in."

MATTHEW 9:37

"The results of splitting the world
into secular and sacred sections
have become disastrous,"
notes Thomas Carruthers.
"We have fenced off a nice little area
of life and labeled it religion.
That is not enough.
We must take Christ into our factories,
schools, newspaper offices,
businesses, homes, everywhere."
Carruthers's point is an important one.
Jesus did not intend
that only certain disciples be involved
in bringing in the "harvest."
He intended all of us to be involved.

To what extent am I splitting my world
into "secular" and "sacred" sections?
How might I be more effective
in taking Christ into "factories,
schools, newspaper offices, businesses,
homes, everywhere"?

Do what you can with what you have,
where you are.

THEODORE ROOSEVELT

SUNDAY
Advent
Week 2 _____

[John the Baptist began preaching,]
"Turn away from your sins
and be baptized,
and God will forgive your sins."

LUKE 3:3

Legend says that while painting
The Last Supper, Leonardo da Vinci
had a terrible fight with someone.
Afterward, he went to his studio,
picked up his brush,
and prepared to paint the face of Jesus.
To his dismay
he couldn't make a single decent stroke.
He put down his brush,
went to the man he had fought with,
and asked his forgiveness.
Leonardo returned to his studio
and resumed painting the face of Jesus.

Have I ever had an experience
similar to Leonardo's?
What motivates me to repent my sins?

It is one thing to mourn sin
because it exposes us to hell . . .
and another thing to mourn it
because it is wrong and offensive to God.
It is one thing to be terrified,
another, to be humbled.

GARDINER SPRING

[Jesus said to the paralytic,]
"Your sins are forgiven."

LUKE 5:20

Years ago,
Joe Queen drove an ice cream truck.
Attached to it were two brass bells,
which Joe rang by hand
to announce he was in the neighborhood.
On Christmas morning Joe, now retired,
found a cardboard box on his porch.
Inside it were two brass bells,
a box of cookies, and a note saying,
"Twenty-five years ago,
I stole these bells off your truck.
Sorry. Merry Christmas."
Joe said, "If I'd seen him when he left
the bells, I'd have shaken his hand
and told him he was forgiven."

Joe's readiness to forgive is an image
of Jesus' readiness to forgive.
It makes me ask, Why am I hestitant
to forgive or to ask forgiveness?

Forgiveness
is the answer to the child's dream
of a miracle by which
what is broken is made whole again,
what is soiled is again made clean.

DAG HAMMARSKJOLD

TUESDAY
Advent
Week 2 _____

[Jesus said,]
"Your Father in heaven
does not want any of these little ones
to be lost."
                                    MATTHEW 18:14

Talk-show hostess Oprah Winfrey
has a wonderful way with her guests.
Her honesty relaxes them,
and it is not uncommon for her
to cry with them right on the show.
In November 1991 she appeared
before a Senate Judiciary Committee,
on the question of child abuse.
She told the senators:
"I was raped at the age of 9
by a 19-year-old cousin.
I was repeatedly sexually molested
by a family friend after that,
and when I was 14,
I was molested by an uncle.
The violators are still living," she said,
"and my family is aware
of who they are."

How do I handle abuse, past and present,
in my life? How do I treat children?

A child's life is like a piece of paper
on which every passerby leaves a mark.
                              ANCIENT CHINESE PROVERB

[Jesus said,]
"Take my yoke and put it on you,
and learn from me,
because I am gentle and humble in spirit;
and you will find rest.
For the yoke I will give you is easy,
and the load I will put on you is light."

MATTHEW 11:29-30

Roger Bolduc died in Waterville, Maine,
after a long bout with cancer.
Until the end, he regarded his illness
as a gift from God.
Shortly before dying, he wrote:
"Many things
upon which I placed importance
in the past seem trivial now. . . .
God has become so real. . . .
I have always felt close to God,
but feel even closer now. . . .
I can feel God's power—
it's always there. I feel loved."

When do I experience God's presence
most—in times of adversity or in times
of prosperity? How do I explain this?

In the midst of winter,
I finally learned that there was in me
an invincible summer.

ALBERT CAMUS

THURSDAY
Advent
Week 2 _____

[Jesus spoke to the people, saying,]
"John [the Baptist] is Elijah,
whose coming was predicted."

MATTHEW 11:13

Orthodox Jews still place an empty chair
for Elijah at each yearly Seder meal.
They do so, hoping this will be the year
Elijah will return to prepare the way
for the Messiah's coming.
Their practice and their hope is rooted
in two Old Testament episodes.
The first is the description of Elijah
being taken "up to heaven" in a
"chariot of fire" (2 KINGS 2:11).
The second is the promise of God
that Elijah will return again
prior to the Messiah's coming
to prepare the way for him (MALACHI 4:5).
Jesus makes it clear in today's reading,
and elsewhere, that "Elijah has already
come," in the person of John the Baptist
(MATTHEW 17:12).

Advent is like the coming of the Baptist.
It calls us to prepare for the coming
of Jesus. How well am I heeding its call?

Better to do something imperfectly
than to do nothing flawlessly.

ROBERT H. SCHULLER

[Jesus said,] "When John came,
he fasted and drank no wine, and
everyone said, 'He has a demon in him!'
When the Son of Man came,
he ate and drank,
and everyone said, 'Look at this man!
He is a glutton and winedrinker.' "

MATTHEW 11:18-19

A cartoon shows a European hunter
boasting of his marksmanship
to a group of natives on an island.
Just then a duck flies overhead.
"Watch this!" he shouts boastfully.
The gun barks, but the duck flies on!
"My friends," he said in awe,
"you are now witnessing a rare sight.
You are seeing a duck continuing to fly,
even though he is dead!"

The people's response to Jesus
and the hunter's response to the natives
show what happens
when we close our minds to reality.
We see things not as they are,
but as we are. This raises a question:
Might there be an area in my life
where I have closed my eyes to reality?

The heart has a way of talking the mind
into whatever it wants.

SATURDAY
Advent
Week 2 _____

[Jesus said to his disciples,]
"Elijah has already come
and people did not recognize him,
but treated him just as they pleased.
In the same way
they will also mistreat the Son of Man."

MATTHEW 17:12

A popular movie by Ingmar Bergman
is *Winter Light.* One of its characters
is a crippled janitor of a church.
He suffers from constant pain
in his back and in his bones.
Then one day he suffers a new pain:
a mental pain resulting from
his meditations on Jesus' crucifixion.
These meditations lead him to conclude
that Jesus' greatest pain was *mental.*
In spite of having loved so much, healed
so many, and given himself so totally,
many people didn't know about Jesus,
didn't care about him, didn't follow him.
On the surface, Jesus' life and his death
seemed almost useless—a failure.

What message might people's treatment
of the Baptist and of Jesus hold for me?

[Jesus said,] "Do not be afraid of those
who kill the body but cannot kill the soul."

MATTHEW 10:28

*[A man named John
began preaching at the Jordan River.]
People's hopes began to rise,
and they began to wonder whether
John perhaps might be the Messiah.*

LUKE 3:15

Viktor Frankl was a Jewish psychiatrist
when the Nazis arrested him
and sent him to a concentration camp.
In his book *Man's Search for Meaning,*
he describes some of the sufferings
that Jews endured in those camps.
One was the pain of waiting—
waiting to learn the fate of loved ones,
waiting to learn one's own fate,
waiting to be rescued.
The pain of waiting also plagued Jews
in Jesus' time—waiting to be delivered
from the Romans, waiting for the
Messiah to come. This pain affected
Jews in different ways.
Some lost hope; some lost faith.
Others simply watched and prayed.

What is one thing I am waiting for
in my life? How is this affecting me?

*"Be strong and don't be afraid!
God is coming to your rescue."*

ISAIAH 35:4

SPECIAL NOTE

Starting today, the Lectionary readings for
Advent vary from year to year, depending on
what day Christmas falls. To determine which
reflection exercise to use today,

• find the current year,
• read across to the date listed,
• page ahead to that date and begin there.

This will put you in the correct sequence from
now until Christmas. (For example, if the year
is 1995, page ahead to December 18 and begin
there.)

——————————————————— Advent

[Jesus asked his opponents,]
"Where did John's right to baptize
come from: was it from God or man?" . . .
[They puzzled,] "What shall we say?
If we answer, 'From God,' he will say to us,
'Why, then, did you not believe John?'
But if we say, 'From man,' we are afraid
of what the people might do, because they
are all convinced that John was a prophet."
So they answered Jesus, "We don't know."
MATTHEW 21:25-27

In May 1915, the Germans sank
the U.S. passenger ship *Lusitania,*
claiming it was carrying munitions.
U.S. officials denied this and used the
event to get the U.S. into World War I.
Later it was proven that U.S. officials
knew that the ship was carrying arms
but feigned ignorance.

A woman said, "Most people aren't liars;
they just keep truth at a safe distance."
What did she mean, and how might it
apply to my life to some extent?

If you tell the truth,
you have infinite power supporting you;
but if not,
you have infinite power against you.
GENERAL CHARLES GORDON

DECEMBER 13

Advent _____

[Jesus told a parable of two sons.
The older son
refused to help his father
but later changed his mind and did so.
The other son did just the opposite.
Jesus asked,] "Which one of the two
did what his father wanted?"

MATTHEW 21:31

That parable is strikingly similar
to Jesus' parable of the prodigal son,
where the runaway son stands for sinners
who start badly but end well,
and the other son
stands for the scribes and Pharisees
who start well but end badly.

Both parables act as *mirrors*.
That is, they invite me
to look into my heart and ask,
Am I like the son who reformed?
Am I moving closer to God in my life?
Or am I like the other son,
drifting further away from God?
How do I explain my present situation?

If we are not rising upwards
to be an angel,
depend on it, we are sinking downwards
to be a devil.

SAMUEL TAYLOR COLERIDGE (adapted)

DECEMBER 14

_____ Advent

*[When John the Baptist sent envoys
to ask Jesus if he were the expected one,
Jesus replied,] "Go back and tell John
what you have seen and heard:
the blind can see,
the lame can walk, . . .
the deaf can hear,
the dead are raised to life."*

LUKE 7:22

Isaiah foretold that the following signs
would announce the Messiah's arrival:
"The blind will be able to see,
and the deaf will hear.
The lame will leap and dance,
and those who cannot speak
will shout for joy" (ISAIAH 35:5-6).
Jesus presents his miracles
as the signs foretold by Isaiah.
Jesus is the long-awaited promised one.
He is ushering in the Kingdom of God,
foretold by the prophets.

If Jesus asked me what "blindness" or
"deafness" I would like to be healed of,
what answer would I make to him?

*In Jesus all broken lines unite.
In Jesus all scattered sounds
are gathered in harmony.*

PHILLIPS BROOKS

DECEMBER 15

Advent _____

[Jesus said
that John was chosen by God
to prepare the way for the Messiah.
Jesus added,] "John is greater
than any man who has ever lived."

LUKE 7:28

During Caesar's reign in Rome
and Herod's reign in Judea, there developed
among the downtrodden in both nations
an "expectant hope."
It was focused on the coming of a savior
who would champion their cause.
Many Romans thought Caesar Augustus
might be the Roman savior.
But when he died, so did their hope.
In Judea, however, the "expectant hope"
for a savior or "messiah" did not die.
In fact, it grew stronger.
Now Jesus says that John the Baptist
has been sent by God to prepare the way
for the coming of "the Messiah."

What is threatening to keep me
from doing what I ought to do
to prepare for the Christmas celebration
of the Messiah's coming?

Our actions
are the best witnesses of our thoughts.

ANONYMOUS

_____ Advent

[Jesus said,] "John was like a lamp,
burning and shining,
and you were willing for a while
to enjoy his light."

JOHN 5:35

In *The Day Christ Died,*
Jim Bishop tells how Jews
longed for the Messiah's coming.
He describes it in words like this:
"They longed for it
with an eagerness beyond belief.
It was comfort for the weary farmer
as he lay waiting for sleep.
It was the dream of the aged person
nearing the end of life.
It was the thing a small child looked to
a mountain of snow-white clouds to see.
It was the hope of Judea in chains.
It was the dream that made
even the most painful life bearable."

The longing with which Jews
looked forward to the Messiah's coming
invites me to ask, With what kind
of longing do I look forward
to the Savior's coming on Christmas?

Christ is not valued at all
unless he is valued above all.
SAINT AUGUSTINE

DECEMBER 17

Advent ———————————————

This is the list of the ancestors of Jesus. . . .
From Abraham to King David,
the following ancestors . . .
From David to the time when the people
of Israel were taken into exile in Babylon,
the following ancestors . . .
From the time after the exile in Babylon
to the birth of Jesus, the following . . .

MATTHEW 1:1-2, 6, 12

Matthew groups Jesus' ancestors
according to the three major eras
of Israel's "spiritual history":
their call to greatness,
their fall from greatness,
their recall to greatness.
God created God's people to be great.
When they sinned and fell from greatness,
God mercifully restored them.
Israel's "spiritual history" parallels
our own "spiritual history":
God calls us to greatness;
we sin and fall from greatness;
God recalls us to greatness.

How can I repay God for God's mercy?

We are stardust, we are golden—
and we've got to get ourselves
back to the garden.

JONI MITCHELL

———————————————— Advent

[An angel told Joseph in a dream,]
"Take Mary to be your wife. . . .
She will have a son,
and you will name him Jesus—
because he will save his people
from their sins."

MATTHEW 1:20-21

Three teenagers were climbing Mt. Hood.
When a massive blizzard struck,
they made a snow cave to wait it out.
For two weeks they huddled in the cave.
Their only comfort was a pocket Bible,
which they took turns reading aloud.
Finally, on the 16th day,
when they were low on food and hope,
the weather broke. They crawled out
of the cave, barely able to stand.
Looking down the mountain,
they saw a joyous sight: a rescue team.
The situation of the teenagers,
waiting and hoping, gives us an insight
into the situation of believing Jews
before Jesus' birth.
They, too, were low on faith and hope.

What keeps me going when I am low
on faith and hope and tempted to quit?

Prayer infuses the weak with strength
and the fainthearted with courage.

DECEMBER 19

Advent _____

[An angel appeared to Zechariah, saying,]
"Your wife Elizabeth will bear you a son.
You are to name him John. . . .
He will bring fathers and children
together again; . . . he will get
the Lord's people ready for him."

LUKE 1:13, 17

If you haven't heard of
the "Advent Devil," don't be surprised.
Its strategy is to keep a low profile—
so low that you never notice it.
But that doesn't mean it's not there.
It just means its strategy is working.
Its job is to keep you so busy
with Christmas shopping,
party excitement, and holiday activity
that you don't take the time
to reflect on the true meaning
of Christmas.
And so you miss the point of Christmas.
You miss preparing
for the rebirth of Jesus in your heart.

To what extent
is the strategy of the Advent Devil
working in my case?

Why not let Jesus take over your life?
He can do far more with it
than you can.

DECEMBER 20

———————————————— Advent

*God sent the angel Gabriel to a town
in Galilee named Nazareth.*

LUKE 1:26

In your imagination,
picture the human race before
the coming of Jesus
It is under Satan's power and control.
Sin and hopelessness are everywhere.
Into this world
God sent the angel Gabriel to a virgin,
named Mary. Gabriel said to her:
"You will become pregnant
and give birth to a son,
and you will name him Jesus.
He will be great and will be called
the Son of the Most High God.
The Lord God will make him a king,
as his ancestor David was, and . . .
his kingdom will never end!" . . .
And the angel left her.

LUKE 1:31-33, 38

What might have gone through Mary's
mind after the angel left her?

*Let those love now,
who never lov'd before;
let those who always lov'd,
now love the more.*

ANONYMOUS

DECEMBER 21

Advent _____

[Mary greeted her cousin Elizabeth.]
When Elizabeth heard Mary's greeting,
the baby moved within her.
Elizabeth was filled with the Holy Spirit
and said in a loud voice,
"You are the most blessed of all women,
and blessed is the child you will bear!"

LUKE 1:41-42

A shabbily dressed man wandered
into a church during a Mass for children.
He sat down and seemed to fall asleep.
After Mass the children sang a hymn
in honor of Mary.
The hymn ended with these words:
"Mother of Christ, Star of the Sea,
pray for the wanderer, pray for me."
Suddenly the man began sobbing.
When someone went over to him, he said,
"I'm all right! It's just that song.
I haven't heard it since I was a boy,
and I haven't been in a church for years."
That hymn to Mary occasioned
the return of the old man to his faith.
Once again, Mary was a source of grace.

What role does the mother of Jesus
play in my spiritual life?

Mother of Christ, Star of the Sea,
pray for the wanderer, pray for me.

DECEMBER 22

———————————————— Advent

His name is holy;
from one generation to another he shows
mercy to those who honor him.

LUKE 1:49–50

The Little Prince is a fantasy
about an alien stranded on earth.
Naturally, he is frightened.
One earthling who helps him is a fox.
When the two must separate for a while,
the fox insists on setting the exact time
for their next meeting.
When the Little Prince asks the fox
why he wants to set an exact time,
the fox says,
"If I know you're coming at 4 o'clock,
then I'll begin to be happy at 3 o'clock."
Ancient Jews also longed to know
the exact time of the Messiah's coming,
but God chose not to reveal it.

How patiently do I wait
for Jesus' fuller coming into my life?
What is meant by a "fuller" coming?

Lead, kindly Light,
amid the encircling gloom. . . .
I do not ask to see
The distant scene;
one step enough for me.

JOHN HENRY NEWMAN

DECEMBER 23

Advent _____

*[The circumstances surrounding
John the Baptist's birth made people ask,]
"What is this child going to be?"*

LUKE 1:66

The circumstances surrounding
Tom Fleming's youth made people ask,
"What is this child going to be?"
He couldn't read or write and was running
with a gang of young toughs in Detroit.
Forty-two years later,
Tom stood at the side of the president
of the United States to be honored.
He had just completed his 20th year
of teaching disadvantaged teenagers.
Tom Fleming is dramatic proof
that throwaway kids can break the cycle
of drugs and crime—and succeed.

How am I helping throwaway kids
break the cycle of drugs and crime?
What is one thing I might begin to do?

*Each newborn child arrives on earth
with a message to deliver to mankind.
Clenched in his little fist is
some particle of yet unrevealed truth,
some missing clue, which may solve
the enigma of man's destiny. . . .
He must be treated as top-sacred.*

SAM LEVINSON

*"Our God is merciful and tender.
He will . . . guide our steps
into the path of peace."*

LUKE 1:78-79

On Christmas Eve,
during the Franco-Prussian War in 1870,
French soldiers and German soldiers
were facing each other in trenches
a short distance apart.
Suddenly a French soldier stood on top
of the mound of dirt.
He faced the Germans
and began singing "O Holy Night."
Not a shot was fired.
When the French soldier finished,
a German soldier did the same,
singing "From Heaven to Earth Come."
Not a soldier present that Christmas Eve
ever forgot the event.

What lesson might that event hold
for me? For our world?

*The world is large and complex,
and sometimes
there seems to be no sacred ground.
But in tent and palace . . .
and under lighted trees across the lands,
the language of Christmas is universal.*

MARCUS BACH

SEASON OF CHRISTMAS

———————————————————— Christmas

*The Word became a human being
and, full of grace and truth,
lived among us.*   JOHN 1:14

The TV documentary *Dear America*
features 42 wartime letters
by Vietnam veterans.
A letter by Peter Elliott describes
Christmas Eve 1970:
"[After gunners sent flares into the sky
to honor the Savior's birth,]
one of the fire bases
started singing 'Silent Night.'. . . .
It was picked up by . . . everyone. . . .
I'm positive it has seldom been sung
with more gut feeling . . .
a strange and beautiful thing
in this terribly death-ridden land."

What thoughts go through my mind
as I imagine myself to be present,
listening to the soldiers singing?

*God's glory, now, is kindled gentler
than low candlelight
under the rafters of a barn:
Eternal Peace is sleeping in the hay,
and Wisdom's born in secret
in a straw-roofed stable.*

                    THOMAS MERTON

DECEMBER 26

Christmas Season _____

[Jesus said to his followers,]
"For my sake you will be brought to trial
before rulers and kings. . . .
Men will hand over their own brothers
to be put to death. . . .
But whoever holds out to the end
will be saved."

MATTHEW 10:18, 21-22

You can only marvel at Jesus' honesty
in this gospel passage.
He doesn't sugarcoat what to expect
if you follow him.
Worldly wisdom would say,
"They will wine you and honor you."
Jesus says, "They will whip you . . .
[and] hate you" (MATTHEW 10:17, 22).
As William Barclay reminds us, however,
history proves that Jesus was right.
In their heart of hearts, people respond
more to the challenging and the heroic
than to their opposites.

What are my thoughts as I reread Jesus'
words in today's Scripture passage?

Perhaps the Church must learn again
that it won't attract people
by the easy way. It is the call of the heroic
that ultimately speaks to the heart.

WILLIAM BARCLAY (slightly adapted)

——————————— Christmas Season

*[Mary Magdalene found the tomb empty
on Easter morning. Immediately,
she ran to tell] Peter and the other disciple,
whom Jesus loved. . . .
Then Peter and the other disciple
went to the tomb . . . saw and believed.*

JOHN 20:2-3, 8

John is called the disciple
"whom Jesus loved" (JOHN 13:23, 19:26, 20:2, 21:20).
Like Jesus, he grew up in Galilee.
There he worked with his brother James
on his father's fishing boat (LUKE 5:9-10).
Along with James and Peter, John enjoyed
a special friendship with Jesus.
They were the only three disciples
present with him during—
• the raising of a girl to life (MARK 5:37),
• the transfiguration (MARK 9:2),
• the agony in the garden (MARK 14:33).
John was also the disciple to whom
Jesus entrusted his mother (JOHN 19:27).
Tradition says John went to Ephesus
with Mary and died there at age 100.

What might have been one thing
that made Jesus love John
in a special way?

The best mirror is a friend's eyes.
GAELIC PROVERB

46

DECEMBER 28

Christmas Season ————————————

[Saint Matthew says that,
in an effort to kill the child Jesus,
Herod] gave orders to kill all the boys
in Bethlehem and its neighborhood
who were two years old and younger.

MATTHEW 2:16

The slaying of the infants reflects
the pathological state of Herod's mind.
He put to death members of his family,
yet rigidly kept Jewish dietary laws,
such as not eating pork.
This provoked a Roman emperor to joke,
"I'd rather be Herod's pig than his son."
An ancient Jewish historian records
that in the final days of Herod's life,
he ordered leading citizens
from many towns in Judea to be killed.
His sick mind reasoned that
the sorrow at their deaths would offset
the joy at his death.
The order was never carried out.

How do I reconcile God's goodness
at allowing evil rulers to inflict pain
on so many innocent people?

"My thoughts," says the LORD,
"are not like yours, and my ways
are different from yours."

ISAIAH 55:8

DECEMBER 29

_____ Christmas Season

There was a man named Simeon
living in Jerusalem.
He was a good, God-fearing man
and was waiting for Israel to be saved.

LUKE 2:25

Nathaniel Hawthorne was dead.
On his desk was the outline to a play
that he never got a chance to write.
It centered around a mysterious person.
Everyone talked about the person.
Everyone dreamed about the person.
Everyone awaited the person's coming.
But the person never came.
The Old Testament is like that play.
It centers around a person, the Messiah,
for whom everyone was waiting
to come and save Israel.

Some people today are like the people
of Old Testament times,
only they're waiting the return of Jesus.
They wonder how close at hand
that event might be.
What are my thoughts about this?

It is by design
that Jesus hid the last day from us—
so that we'd be on the lookout for him
every day of our lives.

SAINT AUGUSTINE

DECEMBER 30

Christmas Season _____

*[The widow Anna] spoke about the child
to all who were waiting
for God to set Jerusalem free.*

LUKE 2:38

In his novel *The Source*, James Michener
uses this poetic image to portray
Jewish society before Jesus' coming.
Rabbi Asher is strolling in an orchard.
Suddenly he spots an old olive tree.
"Its interior was rotted away,
leaving an empty shell . . .
but somehow the remaining fragments
held contact with the roots,
and the old tree was still vital . . . ;
Asher thought that it well summarized
the state of the Jewish people . . .
much of whose interior had rotted away,
but whose fragments still held their
vital connection with the roots of God,
and that it was through these roots . . .
that Jews could ascertain the will
of God and produce good fruit."

How might I be something like
Jewish society before Jesus' coming?

*When you say a situation or a person
is hopeless, you are slamming the door
in the face of God.*

CHARLES L. ALLEN

DECEMBER 31

_____ Christmas Season

The Word . . .
brought light to mankind.
The light shines in the darkness,
and the darkness has never put it out.

JOHN 1:4-5

An artist painted a picture
of a solitary figure rowing a boat
across a sea at night.
Off in the distance is a solitary star.
The impression you get
as you look at the painting is this:
If the person in that rowboat
ever loses sight of the star in the sky,
the person is lost.
What the painting says about the person
rowing across the sea in the darkness
could be said about us:
If we ever lose sight of the light of Jesus,
we will be utterly lost.

What was the closest I ever came
to losing sight of the light of Jesus?
What might I say to Jesus about it?

Jesus, be a guiding star before me.
Be a soothing wake behind me.
Be a rolling path below me.
Be a flaming hope within me.
Be all these things—now and forever.

ANONYMOUS

JANUARY 1
(Mother of God)
Christmas Season _____

[Shepherds were tending their flocks.
Suddenly God's glory shone about them.
An angel appeared
and told them of Jesus' birth.]
They hurried off
and found Mary and Joseph
and saw the baby lying in the manger.

LUKE 2:16

Columnist D. L. Stewart writes:
"Mothers are the ones
who carry children for nine months.
They are the ones
who learn to sleep on their backs. . . .
They are the ones who sweat, push,
and cry out for pain in the labor room.
Dads pass out cigars.
Mothers are the ones who spend hours
spooning out jars of strained apricots. . . .
Dads lunch at the Racquet Club.
Joseph never passed out cigars
or lunched at the Nazareth Racquet Club,
but you can be sure he appreciated
what Mary went through as a mother."

How deeply do we appreciate
our spouses and what they go through?

Mother is the name for God
in the lips and hearts of little children.
WILLIAM MAKEPEACE THACKERAY

[John said,] "I baptize with water."
JOHN 1:26

The baptism of John
was totally different from
the baptism of Jesus.
John explains the difference this way:
"I baptize you with water to show
that you have repented,
but the one who will come after me
will baptize you with the Holy Spirit"
(MATTHEW 3:11).
John's baptism was simply a *sign*—
of *repentance.*
Jesus' baptism was a *sacrament*—
of *rebirth.*
John's baptism signified
the *rejection* of an old life of sin.
Jesus' baptism signified
the *reception* of a new life of grace:
the incredible life of the risen Jesus.

How well am I nurturing my new life?

When the Church baptizes a child,
that action concerns me,
for the child is thereby connected
to that which is my head, too,
and ingrafted into that body
whereof I am a member.
JOHN DONNE

JANUARY 3

Christmas Season _____

The next day
John saw Jesus coming to him, and said,
"There is the Lamb of God,
who takes away the sin of the world!"

JOHN 1:29

The title "Lamb of God"
calls up two prominent biblical images.
The first is the "sacrificial" lambs
that were offered daily
in the Jerusalem Temple (EXODUS 29).
The second is the "Passover" lamb
that the Israelites offered to God
as they prepared to flee from Egypt.
The Passover lamb's blood
was smeared on all Hebrew houses
to protect them from the angel
who went about slaying Egypt's firstborn
that night (EXODUS 12).
The title "Lamb of God" identifies Jesus
as the new "sacrificial lamb"
and the new "Passover lamb."
His blood will save not just Israel,
but all people from sin (1 CORINTHIANS 5:7).

What return am I making to Jesus for
saving me from sin? Ought I to do more?

Like a lamb . . . he was put to death
for the sins of our people.

ISAIAH 53:7-8

JANUARY 4

——————————— Christmas Season

[When John pointed out the "Lamb of God"
to the two disciples, they went to Jesus
and asked him where he lived.]
"Come and see," [Jesus] answered. (It was
then about four o'clock in the afternoon.)

JOHN 1.35

Ask people where they were
when President John Kennedy was shot.
Many remember not only the exact time
but also the exact place.
Similarly, the two disciples remembered
where they first met Jesus.
One of these two disciples was Andrew;
the other is unnamed.
Many people, however,
think it was John himself,
noting his reference to the exact time and
place of the meeting: four in the afternoon
on the banks of the Jordan.

What is one memorable moment
that I can recall
in my own relationship with Jesus?

Jesus Christ
is the one who is great, little girl.
I knew him long before
them rock-and-roll freaks
made him a superstar.

TV'S ARCHIE BUNKER

JANUARY 5

Christmas Season ⎯⎯⎯⎯⎯⎯⎯⎯

[After discovering Jesus,
Philip brought Nathanael to meet Jesus.
Jesus said of him,] "Here is a real
Israelite; there is nothing false in him!"
Nathanael asked him, "How do you
know me?" Jesus answered, "I saw you
when you were under the fig tree
before Philip called you."

JOHN 1:47-48

What was Nathanael doing
under the fig tree when Jesus saw him?
Some people think he was praying.
Fig trees gave excellent shade and
made good places to sit and pray.
Possibly Nathanael was meditating
on the prophecies about the Messiah.
Possibly he was asking God that
he might see the Messiah face-to-face
before he died.

How convinced am I
that God sees and hears me when I pray?
How might I deepen this conviction?

[Jesus] saw visions we did not see,
and heard voices we did not hear. . . .
He was upon earth, yet he was of the sky.
And only in our aloneness
may we visit the land of his aloneness.

KAHLIL GIBRAN, *Jesus the Son of God*

JANUARY 6

_____ Christmas Season

[Some wise men said,] "We saw his star
when it came up in the east."

MATTHEW 2:1-2

Henry Van Dyke wrote a story about
an imaginary fourth wise man, Artaban.
He was to go with the other three
to search for the newborn king.
Artaban had a pouch of precious gems
as a gift for the baby king.
On his way to join the other three,
he stopped to help a needy person.
The delay was just enough
to cause him to miss the other wise men.
He never did catch them; he kept helping
people and giving away all his gems.
Artaban ended up as a beggar
in a faraway city called Jerusalem.
One day he saw a criminal
being marched off to be executed.
He felt close to this man and was sad
that he couldn't help him.
As the criminal drew near, he turned
to Artaban and said, "Be not sad,
you've been helping me all your life."

How do I imagine Artaban felt
when Jesus said this to him?

"To help the needy is to help me."
MATTHEW 25:40 (paraphrased)

SPECIAL NOTE _____

Starting January 7, the Lectionary readings
vary from year to year. To determine which
reflection exercise to use today,

- find the current year,
- read across to the page indicated,
- turn to that page and begin.

This will put you in the correct sequence from
now until Lent. (For example, if the year is
1995, turn to page 64, "Week after Epiphany:
Saturday" and begin.)

SEASON
OF
EPIPHANY

MONDAY

——————— Week after Epiphany

Jesus heard
that John had been put in prison. . . .
From that time
Jesus began to preach his message:
"Turn away from your sins,
because the Kingdom of heaven is near!"

MATTHEW 4:12, 17

A young man knelt at his bedside.
It was not a sudden impulse
but the result of long soul-searching.
He decided the time had finally come
to open himself totally to Jesus.
There in the darkness of his room,
he expressed sorrow for his sins
and thanked Jesus for making it possible
to have his sins forgiven.
The next day he wrote in his journal:
"Behold, Jesus stands at the door
and knocks. I have heard him
and now he has come into my house.
He has cleaned it and now rules it."

That story and Jesus' words invite me
to ask, What area of my life still needs
to be cleaned and ruled by Jesus?

It is one thing to see the land of peace . . .
and another thing
to tread the road that leads to it.

SAINT AUGUSTINE

TUESDAY

Week after Epiphany —————————

[A huge crowd grew hungry.]
Jesus took the five loaves and the two fish,
looked up to heaven, and gave thanks
to God. He broke the loaves and gave them
to his disciples to distribute. . . .
Everyone ate and had enough.

MARK 6:41–42

This miracle is narrated
by all four of the gospel writers.
Why did it impress them so deeply?
We find the clue in John's gospel.
The day after the miracle, some people
came looking for Jesus. He told them,
"You are looking for me because you ate
the bread and had all you wanted. . . .
Do not work for food that spoils; instead,
work for the food that lasts for eternal
life. . . . The bread that I will give . . .
is my flesh, which I give so that the world
may live" (JOHN 6:26–27, 51). Jesus carried
out this promise at the Last Supper.

At the Last Supper, Jesus said,
"Do this in memory of me" (LUKE 22:19).
How well am I carrying out his request?

If God were to appear to starving people,
he wouldn't dare appear
in any form other than food.

MOHANDAS GANDHI

WEDNESDAY

_____ Week after Epiphany

[One windy night at sea,
Jesus came to his disciples,]
walking on the water. . . .
"It's a ghost!" they . . . screamed. . . .
Then he got into the boat with them,
and the wind died down.
The disciples were completely amazed.

MARK 6:48-51

This remarkable episode comes
after the multiplication of the loaves.
The two events leave the disciples
totally amazed.
They don't understand them.
This much is certain:
After the two events, things are never
the same again for the disciples.
Something beyond their wildest dreams
is starting to happen before their eyes.
Only time will tell them what it is—
and how it all fits together.
In the meantime,
they must trust and be patient.

How trusting and patient am I
when I don't see how things in my life
are fitting together?

The windmill never strays
in search of the wind.

ANDY J. SKLIVIS

THURSDAY

Week after Epiphany ———————

Jesus went to Nazareth,
where he had been brought up,
and on the Sabbath he went as usual
to the synagogue.

LUKE 4:16

Jesus worshiped in two public places:
the synagogue and the Temple.
A synagogue was found in every town.
People gathered there each Sabbath
to hear and ponder God's word.
It was a place of *prayerful learning.*
Jews had only one Temple—
to stress there was only one God.
They gathered there to offer God gifts.
It was a place of *prayerful sacrifice.*
The *Liturgy of the Word,*
as many modern Christians observe it,
mirrors the *synagogue* service.
The *Liturgy of the Eucharist,*
as many modern Christians observe it,
mirrors the *Temple* service.

How faithfully do I gather with others
to worship as Jesus did and
as he instructed his followers to do?

Come, let us bow down and worship . . . ;
let us kneel
before the LORD, our Maker!

PSALM 95:6

FRIDAY

_____ Week after Epiphany

[Jesus] would go away to lonely places,
where he prayed.

LUKE 5:16

In *Seeking the Face of God,*
William Shannon says he made a retreat
at Gethsemani, Kentucky,
in the same hermitage
in which Thomas Merton once lived.
Alongside it was a bed of tiger lilies.
Each evening they'd close their petals
to the outside world for a while.
Each morning, when the sun rose,
they'd reopen their petals to the world.
The rhythmic pattern of the tiger lilies
contains an important lesson for us.
We also need a rhythm in our lives—
of turning *inward* for a while
to pray to God, and
of turning *outward* again,
to work at the tasks God has given us.

How faithful am I to the rhythmic
work-prayer pattern of the tiger lilies—
and Jesus himself?
What is my chief motivation
for maintaining it?

Those who wish to transform the world
must be able to transform themselves.

KONRAD HEIDEN

SATURDAY

Week after Epiphany ————————

*[Some disciples of John the Baptist
became alarmed that his followers
were flocking to Jesus. John replied,]*
*"The bridegroom
is the one to whom the bride belongs;
but the bridegroom's friend,
who stands by and listens, is glad
when he hears the bridegroom's voice.
This is how my own happiness
is made complete. He must become
more important while I become less."*
                                    JOHN 3:29-30

The bridegroom's friend played
an important role in ancient weddings.
One of his jobs was to remain
outside the bridal chamber
until the bridegroom arrived.
John uses this image
to illustrate the relationship
between Jesus and himself.
Now that Jesus has arrived,
it's time for him to recede and rejoice.

How hard is it for me
to recede and rejoice
when another steps into the spotlight?

*Character unfolds its petals
when spotlight and applause die,
and no one is left to praise us.*

SPECIAL NOTE

Ordinary Time begins the Sunday following
Saturday, Week after Epiphany. Therefore,
turn to page 167 and begin with Sunday,
Ordinary Time: Week 1.

SEASON
OF
LENT

_____ Lent

[The LORD says,]
"Repent sincerely and return to me
with fasting and weeping and mourning.
Let your broken heart
show your sorrow."   JOEL 2:12-13

Ash Wednesday
takes its name from the fact that
many Christians anoint their foreheads
with ashes on this day.
The practice
dates back to early Christian times.
It reminds us that, like Jesus,
who died on Good Friday,
we too are marked for death.
It also reminds us
that if we want to rise to eternal life,
as Jesus did, we must repent.
That is, we must let our broken heart
show our sorrow.

What might be an appropriate way
to let my heart show my sorrow
this Lenten season?
Why might this be appropriate?

When the soul has laid down its faults
at the feet of God,
it feels as though it had wings.
                          EUGENIE DE GUERIN

THURSDAY
Lent
Ash Wednesday Week _____

[Jesus said,]
"Will a person gain anything
if he wins the whole world
but is himself lost or defeated?"

LUKE 9:25

The movie *The Closer* is about a man
who has every material thing
he could want—or even dream of.
Yet his life is in tragic disarray.
He is spiritually bankrupt.
The movie ends with the man
standing next to a helicopter pad
on the top of the skyscraper he owns.
As far as the eye can see,
the lights of the city of Los Angeles
sparkle at his feet.
Then suddenly across the movie screen
flash these words of Jesus:
"Will a person gain anything
if he wins the whole world
but is himself lost or defeated?"

What message might *The Closer*
hold for me at this stage in my life?
How might I take the message to heart?

I cannot gauge my wealth
by an inventory of what I have in the bank.
The only valid gauge
is an inventory of what I have in my heart.

FRIDAY
Lent
_____ Ash Wednesday Week

[People asked Jesus,] "Why is it that . . .
your disciples do not fast at all?"
Jesus answered, "Do you expect
the guests at a wedding party to be sad
as long as the bridegroom is with them?
Of course not! But the day will come
when the bridegroom will be taken away
from them, and then they will fast."

MATTHEW 9:14-15

The week after ancient weddings,
Jewish couples were treated
like kings and queens
by friends, neighbors, and relatives.
To fast at this time would be wrong.
Jesus compares
his presence among his disciples
to this joyful time of feasting.
Lent, on the other hand, focuses on
the events that took Jesus from us.
It is the "fasting" time Jesus spoke of
in today's reading.
It is the "preparation" time
for his return in glory at the end of time.

What are some things I might "fast from"
during Lent?

Fast from criticism. . . .
Fast from resentment. . . . Fast from fear.

ARTHUR LICHTENBERGER

SATURDAY
Lent
Ash Wednesday Week _____

[Jesus said,]
"I have not come
to call respectable people to repent,
but outcasts."   LUKE 5:32

A convict in a Kentucky prison
sent a touching prayer that he wrote
to a Jesuit newsletter.
A part of it reads:
"Dear heavenly Father,
I come to you a bent and broken man. . . .
I come to you from prison,
from a place that's called death row
and ask that you take pity, Lord,
on a convict's wretched soul. . . .
Dry these tear-stained eyes;
have mercy on this awful man,
please hear his mournful cries."
JACK JOE HOLLAND
It was for sincere, repentant people,
like Jack Joe, that Jesus came.

What keeps me from composing,
in my journal, a prayer
such as the one Jack Joe composed—
from the depths of his heart?

There is no saint without a past—
and no sinner without a future.
          ANONYMOUS

SUNDAY
Lent
Week 1

*[Jesus] was led by the Spirit
into the desert, where he was tempted
by the Devil.* LUKE 4:1-2

Don Dunn's father owns a garage.
One day a trucker drove in for service.
When it came time for the bill,
the trucker suggested adding
a few "extras," saying,
"The company will pay;
we can split the difference."
Don's father refused.
The driver pushed the point, saying,
"I'm going to be a good customer here.
Why shouldn't we all profit from
the extra-reliable service you offer?"
Don's father said, "That's not my style."
When the driver persisted,
Don's father told him to go elsewhere.
The driver said, "I'll not go elsewhere!
I own a trucking firm,
and I just wanted to be sure
that you were a mechanic I could trust."

What was one of the biggest temptations
I ever faced and overcame?

*[Jesus] can help those who are tempted,
because he himself was tempted
and suffered.* HEBREWS 2:18

MONDAY
Lent
Week 1 _____

"[On judgment day, the King will say,]
'You gave me a drink. . . .'
[The righteous will answer,] 'When . . .?'
The King will reply, '. . . Whenever you
did this for one of the least important . . . ,
you did it for me!' "

MATTHEW 25:35, 37-38, 40

There is a brutal scene in
Victor Hugo's *Notre Dame de Paris*.
The hunchback, named Quasimodo,
is chained to a wheel
and being scourged before a huge mob.
As blood flows from his wounds,
he calls out for water.
The mob responds by jeering him
and pelting him with stones.
Suddenly,
a little girl with a gourd of water
pushes through the crowd and
presses it to his lips.
The girl's loving action makes him do
what his torturers could not do.
A tear rolls down his cheek.

What are my thoughts as I imagine
myself present at this scene?

To ease another's heartbreak
is to forget one's own.
MALCOLM MUGGERIDGE

TUESDAY
Lent
Week 1

[Jesus said,] "When you pray,
do not use a lot of meaningless words,
as the pagans do,
who think that God will hear them
because their prayers are long."

MATTHEW 6:7

Strolling on a beach, a woman spotted
a tiny shell. Picking it up, she said,
"You are a vacation gift from God.
I will take you back with me
and set you on my desk.
There, when things get hectic,
you'll say to me, 'Stop!
Be still, like the axis of a wheel.
Relax a moment in your inner core!' "
This jibes beautifully
with Jesus' instruction in today's reading.
Our best praying often takes place
when we simply sit still and listen—
in the inner core of our being.

How comfortable am I
with the listening phase of prayer?
How can I become more comfortable?

The more faithfully
you listen to the voice within you,
the better you hear
what is sounding outside of you.

DAG HAMMARSKJOLD, *Markings*

WEDNESDAY
Lent
Week 1 _____

[Jesus preached to the people,
asking them to repent,
just as the Ninevites had done, saying,]
"They turned from their sins
when they heard Jonah preach."

LUKE 11:32

An old legend portrays what takes place
outside the gates of heaven
after the world ends.
The last group
of saints and repentant sinners
has just climbed up the golden stairway
that connects earth to heaven.
Everybody is in a festive mood, singing,
and dancing—everyone except Jesus.
He stands alone at the top of the stairs,
looking down toward earth.
He is obviously looking for someone.
When a saint asks him who it is,
Jesus says, "I'm looking for Judas,
hoping he may have had a change of heart
before he died and may still join us."

What point does this legend make?
What does it say to me about a loved one?

There are no hopeless situations;
there are only those
who have grown hopeless about them.

CLARE BOOTH LUCE

THURSDAY
Lent
Week 1

[Jesus said,]
"Ask, and you will receive;
seek, and you will find;
knock, and the door will be opened."

MATTHEW 7:7

Maury Wills won't forget his first day
in a big-league tryout camp.
At the end of the day the coach told him,
"Go back home!
Forget about big-league baseball.
You're too small."
Maury didn't go home,
and he didn't forget about baseball.
For eight years he worked long and hard
in the minor leagues.
"I was close to quitting a hundred times,"
he said, "but I always stuck it out."
The Dodgers
finally gave Maury a chance in 1959.
In 1962, Maury hit .299, stole a record
104 bases, and beat out such stars
as Willie Mays for the National League's
Most Valuable Player award.

What keeps me going
when I'm put down and feel like quitting?

If you only knock long enough . . .
you are sure to wake up someone.
HENRY WADSWORTH LONGFELLOW

FRIDAY
Lent
Week 1 _____

[Jesus said,]
"People were told in the past,
'Do not commit murder;
anyone who does will be brought to trial.'
But now I tell you: whoever is angry
with his brother [or sister]
will be brought to trial."

MATTHEW 5:21-22

A trapped rattlesnake
can become so angry it will bite itself.
That's a good image of what happens
when we let anger control us.
We end up biting ourselves, not our enemy.
We end up destroying ourselves
more than we destroy our enemy.
More and more doctors
are becoming increasingly aware
that at the root of many illnesses
is unresolved anger.
Until the ill person learns to deal
with this anger, no medicine will help.

How do I try to get a handle on anger
when I feel it seething up inside me?

Forgiveness saves
the expense of anger,
the high cost of hatred, and
the waste of energy.

E. C. McKENZIE

SATURDAY
Lent
Week 1

[Jesus said,] "Love your enemies
and pray for those who persecute you. . . .
Why should God reward you
if you love only the people who love you?"

MATTHEW 5.44, 46

Christopher Matthews
is a syndicated columnist and
former aide to House Speaker Tip O'Neill.
In his book *Hardball,*
he quotes an old Texas maxim:
"Hug your friends tight
but your enemies tighter—
hug 'em so tight they can't wiggle."
Matthews, however, gives the maxim
a slightly different spin.
He makes a practical observation
that every politician learns quickly:
"The person who fails to be nice to rivals
throws away golden opportunities.
An astute leader knows
that the opponent in one fight
is often the valued ally in the next."

The politician's motive for "hugging"
a rival invites me to ask, What should be
my motive for "hugging" an enemy?

Always forgive your enemies.
Nothing annoys them so much.

OSCAR WILDE

SUNDAY
Lent
Week 2 _____

While [Jesus] was praying,
his face changed its appearance, and
his clothes became dazzling white. . . .
Peter said to him, "Master,
how good it is that we are here!"

LUKE 9:29, 33

Spiritual writers
sometimes speak of a "moment of grace."
It's a moment when
the border between heaven and earth
appears to fade for a brief second.
It's a moment when,
for a split second of time,
God's presence touches our lives deeply.
It's a moment when,
for a split second of time,
we are blessed with a faint glimpse
of eternity and God's glory.
Such a moment graced Peter, James,
and John in today's reading.
They were never the same after it.

Can I recall a "moment of grace"—
or something akin to it—in my life?
What triggered it? Love? Prayer?

Behind the dim unknown,
Standeth God within the shadow,
keeping watch above his own.
JAMES RUSSELL LOWELL

[Jesus said,] "Do not judge others,
and God will not judge you. . . .
Forgive others and God will forgive you."

LUKE 6:37

A woman's answering machine recorded
a call from a teacher, asking her to call
about her son's irresponsible behavior.
The teacher left no number,
so the woman couldn't let her know
that she had misdialed the call.
A day later another misdialed call
informed "Bob" of a schedule change
for an important business meeting.
Again no number was left.
The woman wondered
what impact these two mistakes
would have on the people involved.
Would the teacher wrongly judge
that the mother didn't care enough
to return the call? Would Bob's boss
wrongly judge him to be irresponsible?
Wrong judgments are so easy to make.

How prone am I to jump to conclusions
and, perhaps, make wrong judgments
that could cause grave harm to others?

Our judgments
are only as good as our information.

ANONYMOUS

TUESDAY
Lent
Week 2 _____

[Jesus rebuked some leaders, saying,]
"They do everything so that people
will see them. Look at the straps
with scripture verses on them
which they wear on their foreheads
and arms, and notice how large they are!"

MATTHEW 23:5

Moses told the people:
"Love the LORD your God
with all your heart,
with all your soul,
and with all your strength.
Never forget these commands. . . .
Tie them on your arms and
wear them on your foreheads
as a reminder" (DEUTERONOMY 6:5-6, 8).
In obedience to this command,
Jews wore tiny straps containing
these commands on the left arm
at the point were it touched the heart
(a sign their heart belonged to God) and
on the forehead (a sign their mind,
also, belonged to God).

Is any of my religious practice done
to impress others?

When we try to make an impression,
that's the impression we make.

ANONYMOUS

[Jesus said,]
"If one of you wants to be great,
he must be the servant of the rest; . . .
like the Son of Man, who did not come
to be served, but to serve."

MATTHEW:20:26-27

Jesus measures greatness differently
from the way modern society does.
Society measures greatness in terms of
the influence one wields,
the position one holds,
the amount of money one makes.
Jesus considers such things irrelevant.
Jesus measures greatness in terms of
the quality of one's service to others:
a nurse's service to patients,
a parent's service to children,
an employer's service
to customers and employees.

Whose measure of greatness
do I tend to follow—society's or Jesus'?
How comfortable am I measuring
another's greatness in this manner? Why?

God selects his own instruments,
and sometimes they are queer ones;
for instance, he chose me
to steer the ship through a great crisis.
ABRAHAM LINCOLN

THURSDAY
Lent
Week 2 _____

*[Jesus told a parable about a rich man
who ignored the plight of a poor man
whom he passed daily outside his gate.
Both died, and their fates were reversed.
The rich man asked Abraham
to send someone to warn his family,
lest they end up as he did, saying,]*
" 'If someone were to rise from death
and go to them,
then they would turn from their sins.'
But Abraham said, 'If they will not
listen to Moses and the prophets,
they will not be convinced even if
someone were to rise from death.' "

LUKE 16:30–31

What is the rich man's sin?
It is *not* that he calls the police
to have Lazarus removed from his gate.
It is *not* that he accuses Lazarus
of being "too lazy to find a job."
It is *not* that he spits on Lazarus
each time he passes him.
What, then, is his sin?

How do I answer that question?

*The great thing in this world
is not so much where we are,
but in what direction we are moving.*
OLIVER WENDELL HOLMES

[Jesus told a parable about a man
who leased his vineyard to tenants
for a share of the crops.
At harvesttime he sent servants
to obtain his share of the crops,
but the tenants abused and killed them.
A second time he sent servants;
again the tenants did the same thing.]
"Last of all [the owner] sent his son. . . .
The tenants . . . killed him." . . .
The chief priests and the Pharisees . . .
knew that he was talking about them.

MATTHEW 21:37-39, 45

Some interpret this story as follows:
The vineyard stands for Israel.
The vineyard owner stands for God.
The tenants stand for Israel's leaders.
The servants stand for God's prophets.
The owner's son stands for Jesus.
One thing that stands out in the story
is *God's patience.* God gave the tenants
three chances to change their ways—
even in the face of their cruel violence.

How grateful am I for God's patience
toward me? What is an example of it?

What can I offer the LORD
for all the LORD's goodness to me?

PSALM 116:12 (adapted)

SATURDAY
Lent
Week 2 _____

[Jesus said, "A father had two sons.
The younger one decided to leave.
So, taking his inheritance, he left.
After spending the money foolishly,
he returned.] He was still a long way
from home when his father saw him . . .
ran . . . and kissed him."

LUKE 15:20

California's Roy Riegels recovered
a Georgia Tech fumble in the 1929 Rose
Bowl and ran 65 yards the wrong way,
eventually costing his team the game.
At halftime Roy expected Coach Price
to tear him apart, but Price merely
put a gentle hand on Roy's shoulder
and said, "The game's only half over.
Give it your all!" Roy did.
When we mess up,
God does exactly what Coach Price did.
God puts a gentle hand on our shoulder
and says, "The game's only half over!
Give it your all!"

How gently do I deal with people
who mess up
and cause me unnecessary hardship?

[Jesus said,] "Learn from me,
because I am gentle and humble in spirit."

MATTHEW 11:29

*[A woman was drawing water at a well.
Jesus said to her,] "Whoever drinks this
water will get thirsty again, but whoever
drinks the water that I will give . . .
will never be thirsty again." . . . "Sir,"
the woman said, "give me that water!
Then I will never be thirsty again."*

JOHN 4:13–15

Actress Helen Hayes says this episode
took place before she was a star:
"I was at a party
feeling very shy because there were
a lot of celebrities around,
and I was sitting in a corner alone
and a very beautiful young man
came up to me and offered me
some salted peanuts and he said,
'I wish they were emeralds.'
as he handed me the peanuts;
and that was the end of my heart.
I never got it back."

The stories of the two women invite me
to ask, Was I ever given a gift in such a
beautiful way that the effect of the
experience is still with me? How?

*The manner of giving
is worth more than the gift.*

PIERRE CORNEILLE

MONDAY
Lent
Week 3 _____

[The people] dragged Jesus out of town,
and . . . meant to throw him over the cliff,
but he walked through the middle
of the crowd and went his way.

LUKE 4:29-30

We usually think of Jesus
as being embraced by loving crowds.
But Jesus was also engulfed
by violent crowds.
Moreover, Jesus told his disciples,
"If they persecuted me,
they will persecute you" (JOHN 16:33).
And they did—how they did!
The apostles were whipped (ACTS 5:40),
Stephen was stoned (ACTS 7:58),
and Paul was beaten eight times
(2 CORINTHIANS 11:24-25).
On the other hand, Jesus told his disciples
not to fear such things, saying,
"Be brave! I have defeated the world"
(JOHN 16:33).

Today's reading invites me to ask,
How does it affect me
when I see my faith cast in a bad light
by the media or in conversation?

[The apostles] were happy . . .
to suffer disgrace for the sake of Jesus.

ACTS 5:41

TUESDAY
Lent
Week 3

*Peter came to Jesus and asked,
"Lord, if my brother keeps on sinning
against me, how many times
do I have to forgive him? Seven times?"
"No, not seven times," answered Jesus,
"but seventy times seven."*

MATTHEW 18:21-22

In the late 1980s
Father Paul Belliveau's parish
was a prison camp of thousands of people
fleeing Salvadoran political persecution.
One Sunday he gave a homily on hatred,
saying, "Jesus refuses to play this game.
He uses love, which forgives enemies."
His homily upset a lot of people who
were suffering greatly from persecution.
After Mass a young man grabbed
the mike and shouted, "Father Paul
said we all have to love and forgive.
Well, that's easy to say."
Another shouted, "Father Paul
doesn't understand our situation."

What strategy do I use to subdue hate—
and to forgive—when hatred attacks me?

*Hatred does more damage
to the person in which it is stored than
to the person on which it is poured.*

ANONYMOUS

WEDNESDAY
Lent
Week 3

[Jesus said in his Sermon on the Mount,]
"Do not think I have come
to abolish the law or the prophets.
I have come not to abolish but to fulfill."

MATTHEW 5:17 (NAB)

Ancient synagogue services began with
a procession of the Scroll of the Law
around the congregation.
This is a small example of the reverence
Jews had for the Law of Moses.
Yet Jesus says he came to fulfill the Law.
The New Testament Greek word *exousia,*
which we translate "authority," means
"power to add or subtract from a thing."
It's this kind of power Jesus claimed and
exhibited in his Sermon on the Mount.
Jesus had to be either a madman or
the Son of God to do what he did.
Small wonder he was always in hot water
with religious leaders.
It took Herculean courage for him
to carry out his Father's mission.

What in my Christian commitment takes
the most courage to carry out? Why?

God's grace within me and
God's strength behind me can overcome
any hurdle ahead of me.

ANONYMOUS

Jesus was driving out a demon. . . .
The crowds were amazed,
but some of the people said,
"It is Beelzebul, the chief of the demons,
who gives him the power."

LUKE 11:14-15

A retired couple was neither
well off nor financially strapped.
Their hobby
was raising chickens and vegetables.
Whenever someone came
to buy fresh eggs or vegetables,
they always charged full market price.
They didn't give a penny discount—
even to friends and neighbors.
This caused some people
to accuse them of being greedy.
Later it was discovered
that the retired couple gave all income
from their vegetables and eggs
to two poor families living nearby.

How prone am I to pass judgment—
especially negative judgment—
on the actions of people?
How might I improve in this area?

If you judge people,
you have no time to love them.
MOTHER TERESA

FRIDAY
Lent
Week 3 _____

[Jesus said,]
" 'Love the Lord your God
with all your heart. . . .
Love your neighbor as you love yourself.'
There is no other commandment
more important than these two. "

MARK 12:30-31

Jeanne Jugan
was a loving 47-year-old woman
in France in 1839.
One day she decided to welcome
into her home an aged blind woman.
Little did Jeanne realize
that this practical act of love
would inspire a worldwide community
of sisters, who would devote their lives
to imitating what she did.
Today the "Little Sisters of the Poor"
share their home and their love
with the elderly in 30 countries.
Their practical, everyday love
has already embraced a million people.

What is one way my own everyday love
could become more practical,
especially when it comes to the elderly?

The test of our love for God
is the love we have for one another.

AUTHOR UNKNOWN

[Jesus said,]
"Everyone who makes himself great
will be humbled,
and everyone who humbles himself
will be made great."

LUKE 18:14

A mighty lion caught a puny mouse.
The mouse cried, "Spare me, great one!
Someday I may be able to help you."
The lion roared with laughter at the idea.
The idea amused the lion so much
that he decided to free the mouse.
Some time later,
hunters captured the mighty lion.
They tied him to a tree
while they went for a cage.
The tiny mouse happened along,
saw the great lion's predicament,
gnawed through the ropes, and freed him.
This ancient fable
makes an excellent illustration
of Jesus' words in today's Bible reading.

How do I treat someone who is powerless
or held in low regard by most people?

A simple judge of my character
is how I treat a person
who can do absolutely nothing for me.

ANONYMOUS

SUNDAY
Lent
Week 4 _____

*[One day Jesus healed a blind youth.
When the Pharisees asked the parents
of the youth who healed him, they said,]
"Ask him; he is old enough,
and he can answer for himself!"
His parents said this because
they were afraid of the Jewish authorities,
who had already agreed that anyone
who said he believed
that Jesus was the Messiah
would be expelled from the synagogue.*

JOHN 9:21-22

There's an old story
about a boy who asked his father,
"Dad, is it really true
that when you were a boy,
you went to church every Sunday?"
His dad replied proudly,
"Yes, son, I went every Sunday!"
The boy thought a minute and said,
"I'll bet my going every Sunday
won't do me any good either!"

What are my thoughts
as I imagine seeing some things I do
through my child's eyes?

*Children often follow the footprints
their parents thought they'd covered up.*

ANONYMOUS

[A Roman official
asked Jesus to heal his son.
Jesus did.
The official] and all his family believed.
This was the second miracle
that Jesus performed after coming
from Judea to Galilee.

JOHN 4:53-54

Fred Smith was a famous biochemist
at the University of Minnesota.
He was also an agnostic.
One day, to placate a friend,
he attended a religious service.
He disliked the singing and the sermon,
but a Bible passage struck him deeply:
"If you confess that Jesus is Lord and
believe that God raised him from death,
you will be saved" (ROMANS 10:9).
That single passage was the seed
from which grew a dynamic faith.
Smith became a leading advocate
of the Gospel on the Minnesota campus.

The faith stories of the official and of the
biochemist invite me to ask, What was
a key moment in my faith story?

Reason led me to the mountain's base;
faith lifted me to the mountain's top.

ANONYMOUS

TUESDAY
Lent
Week 4 _____

*[There was a pool in Jerusalem
where people came to be healed.
A man who had been sick
for thirty-eight years was lying there.
Jesus asked,] "Do you want to get well?"
The sick man answered, "Sir, I don't have
anyone here to put me in the pool
when the water is stirred up. . . ."
Jesus said to him, "Get up,
pick up your mat, and walk."*

JOHN 5:5-8

Two frogs tumbled into a cream vat.
They struggled for about an hour,
trying to climb up the metal side.
Finally, one frog gave up and drowned.
The other struggled on.
He thrashed and thrashed and thrashed.
Then, suddenly, he found himself
sitting safely on a lump of butter.
It is this kind of perseverance
the person in today's gospel showed.

What keeps me thrashing and thrashing
when no hope is in sight?

*Many of life's failures
are people who did not realize
how close they were to success
when they gave up.*

THOMAS EDISON

[Jesus said,] "The Father loves the Son."
JOHN 5:20

Scripture scholar Dorothy Dawes
was watching Israeli children
splashing about in the Sea of Galilee.
Suddenly one child
called out to his daddy, *"Abba!"*
This word caught her by surprise
and moved her deeply.
It was the ancient word that Jesus used—
and taught us to use—to address God.
It literally means "Daddy."
In other words,
Jesus taught us to address God
the same way he himself did:
with the loving trust of a small child
calling out to a loving parent.

What is one thing
that keeps me from addressing God
with the loving trust of a small child?

God in heaven, when the idea of you
awakes in my heart,
let it awaken
not like a frightened bird
that thrashes about in panic,
but like a child waking from a nap—
its face aglow with trusting smile.
SOREN KIERKEGAARD (free translation)

THURSDAY
Lent
Week 4 _____

[Jesus said,]
"The deeds my Father gave me to do,
these speak on my behalf
and show that the Father has sent me."

JOHN 5:36

A high school student asked the pastor
of a church in Plano, Texas,
what he must do to join his church.
"Why do you want to join *this* church?"
the pastor asked.
"Well," said the student, "my friends
belong to a lot of different churches,
but those who belong
to *this* church stand out.
They're the ones I respect most.
I've been looking for a church to join.
When I saw
how the kids in this church acted,
I decided I wanted to join it."
Jesus often spoke of good example
and its power to draw others.

By watching me closely, would someone
be drawn to join the church I belong to?

The flower does not bear the root,
but the root the flower. . . .
The rose is merely the evidence
of the vitality of the root.

WOODROW WILSON

FRIDAY
Lent
Week 4

[Some people said of Jesus,]
"When the Messiah comes,
no one will know where he is from.
And we all know
where this man comes from." . . .
Jesus said in a loud voice,
"Do you really know me
and know where I am from?"

JOHN 7:27-28

Igor Gouzenko was a staff member
of the Soviet Embassay in Ottawa in 1945
when he decided to defect.
He took with him secret documents
exposing a Russian spy ring.
The Canadians didn't believe his story.
It was too incredible.
Only later, by a chance happening,
did the Ottawa police realize
that everything he said was true.
Jesus, too, knew the frustration
of dealing with people
who found him and his message
"too incredible" to believe.

What is "too good to be true"
about Jesus and his message?

Feed your faith
and your doubts will starve to death.
E. C. McKENZIE

SATURDAY
Lent
Week 4 _____

[After Jesus finished speaking,
some people said,] "He is the Messiah!"
[Other people refused to accept
that this could be true.]
So there was a division in the crowd.

JOHN 7:41, 43

President Andrew Jackson
offered a pardon to a prisoner
who had been completely rehabilitated.
The prisoner refused to accept it, saying,
"My debt to society is too great!
I don't deserve to be pardoned!"
Nothing Jackson—or anyone else—said
could change his mind.
He wanted to hear no more about it.
Many people in Jesus' time
were like the prisoner.
Nothing Jesus—or anyone else—said
could change their minds.
They wanted to hear no more about it.

How wedded am I to my own views?
How open am I to discuss them?

Who knows not
and knows not he knows not,
he is a fool—shun him. . . .
Who knows and knows he knows,
he is wise—follow him.

ARABIC SAYING

[Jesus] called out in a loud voice,
"Lazarus, come out!" He came out.
JOHN 11:43-44

A humorous story about Robert Ingersoll,
the famous 19th-century agnostic,
relates to today's Bible passage.
According to the story,
Ingersoll suggested
to an audience of believers
that Jesus' words, "Lazarus, come out!"
were simply a prearranged cue
to have Lazarus (who feigned death)
strut forth gloriously from the tomb.
Emphasizing his point, Ingersoll said,
"Why did Jesus say, *'Lazarus,* come out!'
Why didn't he just say, 'Come out!'
A man in the audience shouted,
"Because if my Master had said that,
every person in that there cemetery
would have come out!"

Apocryphal or not, the Ingersoll story
clarifies the point of the Lazarus story:
All the faithful will rise someday.
What are some of the reasons
I believe this to be true?

Dust thou art, to dust returnest,
Was not spoken to the soul.
HENRY WADSWORTH LONGFELLOW

MONDAY
Lent
Week 5 _____

*[Some religious leaders wanted to stone
an adultress. Jesus] bent over . . .
and wrote on the ground. . . . They all left,
one by one, the older ones first.*

JOHN 8:8–9

In his book *Now I See,*
Arnold Lunn notes that for centuries
people have wondered what Jesus wrote
in the dust with his finger. He writes,
"Had Tolstoy invented that touch,
Christ would have written
something very telling . . . but nothing
half so telling as the silence of John."
Jesus' silent action in today's reading
is sometimes called an "action" parable.
That is, Jesus makes an important point
more by what he does than what he says.
Other action parables include
the times Jesus ate with sinners and
washed the feet of his disciples
(LUKE 5:29, JOHN 13:5).

Today's reading invites me to ask,
What am I saying to others by my actions?
Do they say, "This person's a Christian"?

*One must not only preach a sermon
with his voice,
he must preach it with his life.*

MARTIN LUTHER KING, JR.

[Jesus said of his Father in heaven,]
"I always do what pleases him."

JOHN 8:29

In his book *The Will-Power Problem*,
John Sherrill tells how he gave in
regularly to a certain temptation.
He always resolved that it would be
the last time. It never was.
When John realized its hold on him,
he sought help from a psychiatrist.
When this failed, he turned to Scripture.
A passage from Joshua 24:15
helped him change things. It reads:
"Decide today whom you will serve."
Sherrill understood the passage
as saying, "Make up your mind now!
Don't wait until you're being tempted.
Then it'll be too late."

Jesus' words about doing what pleases
his Father, and Sherrill's strategy
for doing this, invite me to ask,
What is my strategy when I am tempted
to do my will—not God's?

Earthly props are useless,
On Thy grace I fall;
Earthly strength is weakness,
Father, on Thee I call.

JOHN OXENHAM

WEDNESDAY
Lent
Week 5 _____

[Jesus said,] "If you obey my teaching . . .
you will know the truth,
and the truth will set you free."

JOHN 8:31-32

A college girl asked her mother, "How can
you be sure Jesus' teachings are true?"
Her mother's response surprised her:
"You can be convinced in only one way,"
her mother said, "by living them.
If you live Jesus' teachings,
they will speak to your heart
and tell your heart that they are true."
Her mother went on to explain:
"For example, if you forgive enemies,
you will eventually discover
that this is the true thing to do.
And if you don't judge others rashly,
you will eventually discover
that this is the true thing to do."
The mother's remarkable response
is precisely the point
that Jesus makes in today's reading.

Can I recall experiencing the truth
of Jesus' teachings? When? How?

To be convinced of the eternal truths,
do not augment your arguments,
but weed out your passions.

BLAISE PASCAL

THURSDAY
Lent
Week 5

[Jesus said solemnly to the people,]
"Before Abraham was born, 'I Am'."
Then they picked up stones to throw at him.
JOHN 8:58-59

The sacred Hebrew expression "I Am"
is hard to render in English.
Often found in John (6:20; 8:24, 28)
and in Mark (14:62) and Matthew (14:27),
it is a Hebrew identification for God.
(Recall the "burning bush" episode,
where Yahweh [God] says to Moses,
"I am who I am. You must tell them:
'The one who is called I AM
has sent me' " [EXODUS 3:14].)
By applying the expression to Jesus,
gospel writers place him with Yahweh.
It is an expression of divinity.
And the Jews understood it as such.
That's why they picked up stones
to throw at Jesus.
They considered his words blasphemy,
which was to be punished
in this manner (LEVITICUS 24:16).

What are my thoughts as I imagine myself
present at this remarkable event?

I am amazed at the sayings of Jesus. . . .
[They] turn the world upside down.
KATHARINE BUTLER HATHAWAY

FRIDAY
Lent
Week 5 _____

[The people shouted at Jesus,]
"You are only a man,
but you are trying to make yourself God!"

JOHN 10:33

The British historian H. G. Wells
(not a Christian) regarded Jesus
as the world's greatest teacher.
The British theologian C. S. Lewis
considers Wells's evaluation of Jesus
inconsistent with his belief about Jesus.
His point is that you could never call
a man who claimed equality with God
"the world's greatest teacher."
You could call him a fool, a madman,
or a devil, but never a great teacher.
When it comes to Jesus, Lewis says,
you can't have your cake and eat it too.
Only four choices are open to you.
Jesus was either a fool to be pitied,
a madman to be shunned,
a devil to be stoned, or
the Lord to be adored.

Why would I never call Jesus a fool,
a madman, or a devil?

When we have traveled all ways,
we shall come to the End of all ways,
who says, "I am the way."

SAINT AMBROSE

*[The High Priest Caiaphas
said to a meeting of the Jewish Council,]
"Don't you realize that
it is better for you to have one man
die for the people, instead of having
the whole nation destroyed?"*

JOHN 11:50

Caiaphas' remark has been called
the most ironic statement in Scripture.
What the High Priest said was true,
but in a way far different
from what he actually meant.
He meant to say that it was better
to have Jesus die than to have
the Romans destroy the nation of Israel.
But his statement was true
in a more dramatic and profound way.
It was true in the sense that
had Jesus not died, the entire human race
would have perished because of sin.

Have I ever knelt
and thanked Jesus from the heart
for having saved us? For having saved me?

*All my theology
is reduced to this narrow compass,
"Jesus Christ came into the world
to save sinners."*

ARCHIBALD ALEXANDER

SUNDAY
Lent
Week 6 —————————————

Jesus cried out in a loud voice,
"Father! In your hands I place my spirit!"
He said this and died.

LUKE 23:46

Dietrich Bonhoeffer was executed
by the Nazis shortly before Easter.
The prison doctor said of his death:
"I saw Pastor Bonhoeffer . . . kneeling
on the floor, praying fervently. . . .
I was most deeply moved
by the way this lovable man prayed,
so devout and so certain that God heard
his prayer. At the place of execution,
he . . . climbed the steps to the gallows,
brave and composed.
His death ensued after a few seconds.
In the almost fifty years . . . as a doctor,
I have hardly ever seen a man die
so entirely submissive to the will of God."
EBERHARD BETHGE, *Dietrich Bonhoeffer*

What are some of my concerns
as I imagine myself
having only a few minutes left to live?

Is death a leap into a void?
Of course not.
It is to throw yourself
into the arms of the Lord.
PEDRO ARRUPE, S.J.

[Jesus was eating
at the home of Lazarus, Martha, and Mary.
When Mary poured expensive perfume
over Jesus' feet, Judas complained,]
"Why wasn't this perfume sold . . . and the
money given to the poor?" He said this,
not because he cared about the poor,
but because . . . he carried the money bag
and would help himself from it.

JOHN 12:5-6

William Barclay
says of Mary's anointing of Jesus' feet:
"Judas had just seen an action
of surpassing loveliness;
and he called it extravagant waste.
He was an embittered man
who took an embittered view of things."
Judas' reaction
illustrates an important point:
We tend to view situations
not as they really are, but as we are.
We filter them through the prism
of our own positive or negative thinking.

What is one way
that my thinking has been influenced
by this program of daily meditation?

We become that which we think.
BUDDHA

TUESDAY
Lent
Week 6 _____

[At the Last Supper, Jesus became]
deeply troubled and declared openly,
"I am telling you the truth:
one of you is going to betray me."
The disciples looked at one another,
completely puzzled about whom he meant.
JOHN 13:21-22

What puzzles us
is that Jesus' disciples didn't have a clue
about Judas' plan to betray the Master.
How could they have lived so close
to Judas and have been so blind
to what was going on inside him?
Two observations come to mind.
First, our external words and actions
may deceive others,
but they will never deceive God.
Second, the day will come when
everyone will know what is in our heart.
For it is a law of human nature
that what is in our heart has a way
of translating itself into action.

What is one thing in my heart
that I don't want translated into action?

Character
may be manifested in great moments,
but it is made in small ones.
PHILLIPS BROOKS

During the meal Jesus said, ...
"One of you will betray me." ...
Judas, the traitor, spoke up.
"Surely, Teacher, you don't mean me?". ...
Jesus answered, "So you say."

MATTHEW 26:21-25

Judas was able to conceal his plan
from the others but not from Jesus.
And this helps us to see
how gently God deals with sinners.
One of the mysteries of life
is the tremendous respect
God accords to human free will.
God doesn't force us to change.
God invites us to change,
giving us opportunity after opportunity
to open our hearts to grace's power.
Jesus accorded the same respect to Judas.
He made Judas the group's treasurer.
He reserved a place of honor for him
at the Last Supper.

What is one example of how God
has dealt gently with me?

"Here is my servant. ...
I have filled him with my spirit. ...
He will not break off a bent reed
nor put out a flickering lamp."

ISAIAH 42:1, 3

THURSDAY
Lent
Week 6 _____

The Lord Jesus,
on the night he was betrayed,
took a piece of bread,
gave thanks to God, broke it, and said,
"This is my body, which is for you."

1 CORINTHIANS 11:23–24

In 1985 all the TV news programs
showed footage of a woman pinned
beneath a fallen crane in New York City.
Doctors fought to keep her alive
until a larger crane could be brought in
to lift the fallen crane.
They gave her fluids, blood transfusions,
and massive doses of painkiller.
Then came a dramatic moment.
The woman had a request of her own.
She asked for
the Body of Christ in Holy Communion.
This, too, the TV cameras showed.
Eventually the woman was freed
and rushed to a hospital,
where a team of doctors saved her life.

When I imagine I am the injured woman
beneath the fallen crane,
what thoughts go through my mind
as I receive the Body of Christ?

Whoever eats this bread will live forever.

JOHN 6:51 (NRSV)

Pilate handed Jesus over to them to be
crucified. So they took charge of Jesus.
He went out, carrying his cross,
and came to "The Place of the Skull." . . .
There they crucified him . . . . Then he
bowed his head and gave up his spirit.

JOHN 19:16-18, 30

A Protestant minister
was preparing for Holy Week services.
He set up a ladder
so that he could drape a black cloth
over a cross in front of his church.
After he had climbed the ladder,
he tossed the cloth over the cross.
As he did, the ladder tipped.
Frantically, he grabbed the vertical bar
of the cross, saving himself
from a serious fall.
Afterward he confided to a friend,
"That experience helped me appreciate
in a new way how I had been saved
by the cross of Christ."

Can I recall a time when something
helped me appreciate better how Jesus
saved—and continues to save—me?

Nothing in my hand I bring,
Simply to Thy cross I cling.

AUGUSTUS TOPLADY, "Rock of Ages"

SATURDAY
Lent
Week 6 _____

Two men in shining clothes said,
"[Jesus] is not here; he has been raised."
LUKE 24:6

What happened next is history.
Jesus began appearing to his disciples.
He was more radiant
than they had ever seen him.
Suddenly the power of Easter
began to work miracles in their lives:
They ceased being despairing men
and became daring missionaries.
Off they went to preach the Good News.
And everywhere they preached,
the power of Easter worked miracles
in people's lives.
They believed again after doubting.
They hoped again after despairing.
They loved again after hating.
The power of Easter continues
to work miracles in people's lives
wherever it is preached and wherever
people open their hearts to it.

How can I open my heart more fully
to the power of Easter—the power
of the risen Jesus at work in our world?

Immortal hope dispels the gloom!
An angel sits beside the tomb.
SARAH FLOWERS ADAMS

SEASON
OF
EASTER

SEASON
OF
EASTER

Easter

[When John looked into the empty tomb,]
he saw and believed. JOHN 20:8

The good news of Easter
is that Jesus has triumphed
over sin and evil—
and so will we if we open our hearts
to his Easter power.
The good news of Easter
is that every Good Friday in our lives
can be turned into an Easter Sunday.
The good news of Easter
is that nothing can defeat us anymore—
not pain, not sorrow, not even death.
The good news of Easter
is that Jesus will work a miracle
in our lives on this very day
if we will but open our hearts
to his Easter power.

What miracle might I ask Jesus
to work in my life this Easter day?
How might I open my heart,
in a special Easter way,
to let the risen Jesus do this?

The story of Easter
is the story of God's wonderful window
of divine surprise.

CARL KNUDSEN

MONDAY
Easter
Week 1 _____

*[Jewish leaders told the men guarding
Jesus' tomb,] "Say that his disciples
came during the night and
stole his body while you were asleep."*

MATTHEW 28:12-13

The coffin of President Abraham Lincoln
has been opened twice since his death.
The first time was in 1887,
twenty-two years after its burial.
Rumors circulated that the coffin
did not contain Lincoln's body.
It was opened and the body in it
was proven to be Lincoln's.
Fourteen years later,
the same rumors circulated again.
Again the coffin was opened and again
the body was proven to be Lincoln's.
Similar rumors circulated
about the body of Jesus after his death.
The only difference was
that Jesus' body was not in the tomb.
Now the rumors concerned
what happened to it.

What assures me that the body of Jesus
was indeed raised—and not stolen?

*Jesus impacted the lives
of his followers more powerfully
after his death than before it.*

[Jesus appeared to Mary Magdalene,
but she did not recognize him at first.]
Jesus said to her, "Mary!"
[Only then did she realize it was Jesus.]
JOHN 20:16

A trait of the Easter stories
is the failure of Jesus' disciples
to recognize him when he first appeared.
This trait hints at
the nature of Jesus' resurrected body.
Resurrection isn't resuscitation.
It isn't restoration to our former life,
but a quantum leap into a new life.
The body of Jesus that rose on Easter
was infinitely different from the body
that Jesus possessed in his lifetime.
It was transformed; it was glorified.
Paul likens the body
before resurrection to a seed
and after resurrection to a plant
(1 CORINTHIANS 15:37).

What assures me that I will be raised
to new life someday, as Jesus was?

If seeds in the black earth
can turn into such beautiful roses,
what might the heart of man become
in its long journey to the stars?
GILBERT K. CHESTERTON

WEDNESDAY
Easter
Week 1 _____

*[Two disciples were returning home
on Easter. Jesus approached and joined
them, but they didn't recognize him.]
As they came near the village . . .
Jesus acted as if he were going farther;
but they held him back, saying,
"Stay with us [and join us at supper]. . . ."
He sat down to eat with them,
took the bread, and said the blessing; . . .
he broke the bread and gave it to them.
Then . . . they recognized him.*

LUKE 24:28-31

That episode dramatizes what William
Barclay calls the *courtesy* of Jesus.
Jesus doesn't *force* himself on us.
He waits for an invitation from us.
The greatest and the most perilous gift
we possess is our free will.
We can use it to invite Jesus
into our lives or to let him pass us by.

What is one concrete way
that I can invite Jesus into my life?

*["People will ask, 'Lord, when did we]
see you a stranger and welcome you
in our homes . . . ?' The King will reply, . . .
'Whenever you did this for one of
the least . . . of mine, you did it for me!' "*

MATTHEW 25:38, 40

[Jesus appeared in Jerusalem.
His disciples] were terrified, thinking
that they were seeing a ghost. . . .
Then he opened their minds to understand
the Scriptures, and said to them,
"This is what is written:
the Messiah must suffer and
must rise from death three days later."
LUKE 24:37, 45-46

In his book *But That I Can Believe,*
John Robinson tells how the disciples
must have felt on Good Friday night:
"Jesus was someone they had known and
loved and lost. . . . It was all over. . . .
Then it happened. . . . He came to them.
The life they had known and shared was
not buried with him, but alive in them.
Jesus was not a dead memory,
but a living presence."
Today's Bible reading teaches us
that what starts as an unbearable cross
often ends as an incomparable blessing.

What is one cross I carry right now?
What is one way it might possibly
become a blessing in disguise?

Death and Sorrow, earth's dark story,
To the former days belongs.
WILLIAM J. IRONS

FRIDAY
Easter
Week 1 _____

[Jesus appeared on the shore as Peter
and some disciples were returning
from a bad night of fishing. Jesus said,]
"Throw your net out on the right side
of the boat, and you will catch some."
So they threw the net out
and could not pull it back in,
because they had caught so many fish.

JOHN 21:6

Children's Letters to God: The New
Collection by Stuart Hample and Eric
Marshall contains this delightful letter:
"God:
the bad people laghed at noah—
you make an ark on dry land you fool.
But he was smart he stuck with you.
that's what I would do.   Eddie"

Eddie's willingness to stick with God
(even though people may "lagh" at him)
and the disciples' willingness
to stick with Jesus (even though
they caught nothing all night)
invite me to ask,
How willing am I to stick with Jesus—
even though people may "lagh" at me?

The LORD says, . . . "I will bless
the person who puts . . . trust in me."

JEREMIAH 17:5, 7

*Last of all, Jesus appeared to
the eleven disciples. . . . He said to them,
"Go throughout the whole world
and preach the gospel to all mankind."*

MARK 16:14-15

In his book *God's Smuggler,*
Brother Andrew, a Dutch missionary,
tells how he used to smuggle Bibles
into Communist countries
before the fall of the Iron Curtain.
He transported them concealed
in the panels of Fiats and Volkswagens.
"You'd be amazed," he says,
"how many pocket-sized Bibles
you can get in a VW Beetle.
My personal record is 800."
Brother Andrew risked
up to three and a half years in prison
if he got caught.

Jesus' command to go "throughout
the whole world and preach the gospel"
and the risk Andrew took to do this
invite me to ask, What have I risked
in the past to carry out Jesus' command?
What am I risking right now?
What might I risk in the future?

Christianity is a battle, not a dream.

WENDELL PHILLIPS

SUNDAY
Easter
Week 2 _____

*[The apostle Thomas was absent
when Jesus appeared to the disciples;
and he refused to believe, saying,]
"Unless I see the scars of the nails . . .
and put my finger in those scars . . .
I will not believe." [Later Jesus dealt
tenderly with Thomas and he believed.]*

JOHN 20:25

Katherine Gordy Levine
is a professor at Columbia University.
She and her husband have dealt
with foster children all their lives.
Her book *When Good Kids Do Bad Things*
tells how a "good kid," the Dalai Lama,
future Tibetan spiritual leader, did a "bad
thing." He went into the palace garage,
"borrowed" one of his country's four cars,
and smashed it into a tree.
Today's reading tells how another
"good kid" did a "bad thing."

How do I react when a "good kid"
does a "bad thing"? How do I decide
how I should react in such a case?

*Every parent is at some time
the father of the unreturned prodigal,
with nothing to do
but keep his house open to hope.*

JOHN CIARDI

[Jesus said to Nicodemus,]
"No one can enter the Kingdom of God
unless he is born of water and the Spirit.
A person is born physically
of human parents,
but he is born spiritually of the Spirit."

JOHN 3:5-6

Water is a symbol of *purification.*
It washes things and makes them new.
Being born of water
means receiving a new *past:*
being cleansed of sinfulness.
Spirit is a symbol of *transformation.*
Spirit transforms; it re-creates.
Being born of the Spirit
means receiving a new *future:*
being transformed into God's children.
Baptism involves
doffing an *old* life of sin and
donning a *new* life in Christ.

In what sense
is baptism *not* a static event
but an ongoing, never-ending process?
Practically, what does this mean?

The person
who isn't busy being born
is busy dying.

BOB DYLAN (slightly adapted)

TUESDAY
Easter
Week 2 _____

[Jesus said to some skeptical people,]
"You do not believe me when I tell you
about the things of this world;
how will you ever believe me, then,
when I tell you
about the things of heaven?"

JOHN 3:12

Scientist Edward Stein was informed
about the things of the world, but
uninformed about the things of heaven.
This led him to meditate deeply on God.
At first he thought of God as "it";
then he thought of God as "he."
Finally, he began thinking of God as
"the Mysterious Spirit that heals us . . .
[and] evokes tenderness and forgiveness
and hope in us." Stein concluded,
"I don't know, but I trust this love,
I sense this presence.
I have felt the power."
Stein learned what we all must learn:
Unless we turn to Jesus and trust him,
we remain much in the dark about God.

What are some major things
that Jesus has taught me about God?

[Jesus said,] "Whoever has seen me
has seen the Father."

JOHN 14:9

*God loved the world so much
that he gave his only Son,
so that everyone who believes in him
may not die but have eternal life.*

JOHN 3:16

Someone called today's reading
"the Bible within the Bible."
This is because it sums up
the entire biblical message,
affirming the two major biblical truths.
First, God is a "saving God."
Some "Christians" give the impression
that God is more interested
in condemning than in saving.
Nothing could be farther from the truth.
Second, God's initiative to save us
was motivated by God's infinite love—
a love so utterly incredible and mysterious
that God "gave his only Son."

What is my own image of God?
To what extent do I tend to image God
more as a taskmaster than a lover?

*The atheist
staring from his attic window
is often nearer to God
than the believer
caught up in his own false image of God.*

MARTIN BUBER

THURSDAY
Easter
Week 2

Whoever believes in the Son
has eternal life;
whoever disobeys the Son
will not have life.

JOHN 3:36

Most people who turn on a television set
don't know how it works.
But they don't deny that it works.
The image on the screen tells them that.
Most people who drive a car
don't know how it works.
But they don't deny that it does.
The motion of the car tells them that.
In the same way, most people
don't know how faith in Jesus works.
But they don't deny that it does.
The change in their lives tells them that.
Without faith in Jesus,
they could never do the things
they now do.

What is one way faith in Jesus
empowers me to do something
that I could never do without faith?

In our hearts enthrone him;
There, let him subdue
All that is not holy,
All that is not true.

C. NOEL

[At Jesus' request,
a boy gave him some bread and fish.]
Jesus took the bread, gave thanks to God,
and distributed it to the people. . . .
He did the same with the fish,
and they all had as much as they wanted.

JOHN 6:11

Two people were on a train in France.
The older passenger had the Bible open
to the story of the loaves and fishes.
Curious, the younger said to him,
"Pardon me, sir, do you believe
that story, or are you just reading it?"
"I believe it!" he said. "Don't you?"
"No!" said the younger. "I'm a scientist
and that story conflicts with science."
Just then, the train slowed.
"This is my station," said the younger.
"Nice talking to you, Mr. . . ."
"Pasteur," said the older, "Louis Pasteur."
The younger was shocked;
he had just been speaking
with one of the world's top scientists.

How do I handle faith questions when
they seem to conflict with science?

A little science and faith is far;
A lot of science and faith is near.

ANONYMOUS

SATURDAY
Easter
Week 2 _____

*[The disciples were crossing the lake
at night when a storm blew up.
Jesus came to them across the water.
They were utterly terrified.] "Don't be
afraid," Jesus told them, "it is I!"*

JOHN 6:20

A woman had been meditating regularly
with a group for several months.
One morning, she shared the following:
"I've gotten so much from this,"
she began. "But lately, I've begun to fear
where Jesus might be leading me.
Is he going to ask some great sacrifice
of me?"
An older woman, who had been listening
intently, said, "Susan, don't be afraid!
I once felt the same way you feel now.
And Jesus was, indeed, leading me—
just as he *is* clearly leading you also.
As a result, now I'm doing things
I never dreamed I'd do.
But it's filled me with a joy and a peace
that I never dreamed existed."

Do I ever feel Jesus is leading me?
Do I ever fear Jesus might ask
some great sacrifice of me?

What can I fear when I am with God?
BROTHER LAWRENCE

[The disciples had fished all night.]
As the sun was rising, Jesus stood
at the water's edge, but the disciples
did not know that it was Jesus.
Then he asked them, "Young men,
haven't you caught anything?"
"Not a thing," they answered.
He said to them, "Throw your net out
on the right side of the boat,
and you will catch some." So they threw
the net out and could not pull it back in,
because they caught so many fish.

JOHN 21:4-6

Harry Lloyd once said,
"I thank God that I live in a country
where dreams can come true,
where failure sometimes
is the first step to success."
We can say the same about our faith—
as today's gospel story illustrates.

Can I recall a time when some failure
led me to discover Jesus and his help?

Make ready for the Christ,
whose smile, like lightning,
sets free the song of everlasting glory
that now sleeps in your paper flesh,
like dynamite.

THOMAS MERTON

MONDAY
Easter
Week 3 ⎯⎯⎯⎯⎯⎯⎯⎯⎯

[Jesus said,] "Do not work for food
that spoils; instead, work for the food
that lasts for eternal life.
This is the food
which the Son of Man will give you."

JOHN 6:27

Four billion people live on Earth.
Half a billion suffer from chronic
physical hunger or malnutrition.
But a more frightening statistic
about hunger and malnutrition is this:
Perhaps, three billion people
suffer from chronic
spiritual hunger or malnutrition.
It is this hunger
that Jesus refers to in today's reading
when he exhorts the people to seek
not just *body* food but also *soul* food.

Who is someone I know who seems
to suffer from chronic spiritual hunger
and malnutrition? What might be
a "first step" toward helping him or her?

Every human heart—
from a teenager watching MTV
to a cabdriver waiting for a fare—
has a spiritual void
that only Infinite Love can satisfy.

ANONYMOUS

[Jesus said,]
"I am the bread of life. . . .
Whoever comes to me
will never be hungry;
whoever believes in me
will never be thirsty."
JOHN 6:35 (adapted)

Two people in weight-control programs
were reflecting together
on what tends to cause them to overeat.
One person said,
"I've noticed that I always overeat
whenever I am bored or depressed."
The other said, "I do the same thing.
And lately I've begun to wonder.
Could my boredom and depression
be caused by a *spiritual* hunger,
which I then try to satisfy
with *material* food and drink?"

When I am bored or depressed,
what "food and drink" do I turn to?
What might be a better alternative?

The LORD says, . . . "Why spend money
on what does not satisfy?
Why spend your wages and still be hungry?
Listen to me and do what I say,
and you will enjoy the best food of all."
ISAIAH 55:1-2

WEDNESDAY
Easter
Week 3 _____

[Jesus said,]
"I have come down from heaven to do
not my own will
but the will of him who sent me. . . .
What my Father wants is that all
who see the Son and believe in him
should have eternal life."

JOHN 6:38, 40

In his outstanding book
The Great Divorce,
the British theologian C. S. Lewis
divides the world
into two groups of people:
"Those who say to God,
'Thy will be done,'
and those to whom God says,
'All right, then, have it your way.' "

The words of Jesus in today's gospel—
and the twofold category
into which Lewis divides the world—
invite me to ask,
In which category of people
do I most often find myself? Why?

The world
and everything in it that people desire
is passing away;
but he who does the will of God
lives forever.   1 JOHN 2:17

THURSDAY
Easter
Week 3

[Jesus said,] "The prophets wrote,
'Everyone will be taught by God.'
Anyone who hears the Father
and learns from him comes to me."

JOHN 6:45

During the depression,
a room was filled with applicants
for a job opening as telegraph operator.
The drone of conversation competed
with a steady flow of dots and dashes.
The door opened and yet another applicant
entered the room.
He stood there a minute, walked over
to a door marked "Private," and knocked.
A man opened it and said to the others,
"You may all go; we have our applicant."
The others were furious and demanded
an explanation. The man said, "Listen!"
They did. The dots and dashes
kept repeating over and over again,
"If you hear this, come in; the job's yours."
That story reminds us
that God is constantly speaking to us,
but we are not listening.

What are some ways God may be speaking
to me right now? How well am I listening?

Jesus concluded, "Listen, then."

LUKE 8:8

[Jesus said,]
"My flesh is the real food;
my blood is the real drink.
Whoever eats my flesh
and drinks my blood
lives in me, and I in him."
JOHN 6:55-56

A person was asked,
"Why do you believe in miracles?"
The person said, "Because I see them
in the lives of people
who take Jesus at his word."
That reply explains why we gather
on the Lord's Day at the Lord's table
to eat the Lord's Supper
and pray the Lord's Prayer.
It says in an unmistakable way
that faith is real, hope is possible,
and love is alive.
It says that "Christ has died,
Christ is risen, Christ will come again."

Why am I slow to take Jesus at his word?

When people hear us speak God's word,
they marvel at its beauty and power;
when they see what little impact
it has on our daily lives,
they laugh and poke fun at us.
SECOND-CENTURY CHRISTIAN

Many of his followers heard this
[Jesus' teaching about his body
and blood] and said,
"This teaching is too hard. . . ."
[They] would not go with him any more.

JOHN 6:60, 66

Many of us have shared the Lord's Supper
since childhood.
But, if we are honest, we must admit
that this has not brought us
as close to Jesus and one another
as we had hoped that it would. Why?
Perhaps it's because we tend to view
the Lord's Supper as only a *meal:*
a time of receiving.
We tend to forget it is also a *sacrifice:*
a time of giving and of forgiving.
In other words, we will walk with Jesus
in the sunlight of Easter morning
only to the extent that we first walk
with him through the shadows
of Good Friday afternoon.

How faithfully am I walking with Jesus
through the shadows of Good Friday?
How might I remedy my shortcomings?

All that we send into the lives of others,
Comes back into our own.

EDWIN MARKHAM

SUNDAY
Easter
Week 4 _____

"My sheep . . . follow me . . .
and they shall never die.
No one can snatch them away from me."
JOHN 10:27-28

A daughter found this moving prayer
among her father's possessions
after he died:
"I cannot pray, dear Lord.
I cannot find . . .
recovery, health, and peace of mind. . . .
Although You suffered more than I,
this does not help me,
no matter how I try. . . .
Take my feeble frame,
and give me strength. . . .
I need to know
that with Your help we will succeed. . . .
So take my hand,
and let me cling to Thee, and, clinging,
know no harm can come to me."
CHRISTOPHER NEWS NOTES

What thought in the father's prayer
can I relate to best and make my own?

Precious Lord, take my hand . . .
thro' the storm, thro' the night,
lead me to the light. . . . Take my hand,
Precious Lord, lead me home.
THOMAS A. DORSEY

[Jesus said,
"Whoever] does not enter the sheep pen
by the gate . . . is a thief. . . .
The thief comes only in order
to steal, kill, and destroy. I have come
in order that you might have life—
life in all its fullness."

JOHN 10:1, 10

A tourist wanted to see for himself
that sheep won't follow a stranger—
as Jesus said—"because they do not know
his voice" (JOHN 10:5).
He arranged with a shepherd to put on
the shepherd's outer cloak and turban.
Then he went outside to the flock.
He yelled, *"Manah!"* (Arabic for "Come!").
But not a single sheep budged.
Impressed, the tourist asked,
"Will your sheep ever follow anyone
other than you?" "Yes," said the shepherd.
"Sometimes a sheep will get so sick,
it will follow anyone."

How attentively do I listen
for the voice of Jesus, my shepherd?

God is much more anxious
to communicate with us
than we are to listen.

MORTON KELSEY

TUESDAY
Easter
Week 4 _____

[Jesus said,]
"My sheep . . . follow me.
I give them eternal life."

JOHN 10:27-28

A woman on vacation in Israel
was watching a shepherd lead his flock.
Shortly, they came to a shallow stream.
In spite of the shepherd's calls,
the flock grew frightened and froze.
He bent down, gently picked up a lamb,
and carried it across.
When the mother
saw her lamb on the other side,
she waded through the water to join it.
Immediately the others followed.

Can I recall a time when I became
frightened and hesitated to follow Jesus?
What helped me
to overcome my fear and hesitancy?

The LORD is my shepherd;
I have everything I need.
He lets me rest in fields of green grass
and leads me to quiet pools
of fresh water.
He gives me new strength.
He guides me in the right paths,
as he has promised.

PSALM 23:1-3

WEDNESDAY
Easter
Week 4

Jesus said . . . , "Whoever believes in me
believes not only in me
but also in him who sent me. Whoever
sees me sees also him who sent me."

JOHN 12:44–45

John Donne wrote a poem about a person
who is told that God lives
atop a mountain at the end of the earth.
The person travels to the mountain
and begins the long journey up it.
At that very moment, God thinks,
"What can I do to show my people
how deeply I love them?"
God decides to journey down
the mountain and live among the people.
Thus, when the person reaches
the top of the mountain, God is not there.
The person thinks, "God doesn't live here!
Perhaps, God doesn't even exist."
Donne's point is that we often look for
God in the wrong place, forgetting
that God came down from heaven
and resides among us.

Where have I looked for God in the past?
Where am I looking for God now?
Where ought I look for God in the future?

God dwells wherever we let him in.
ANCIENT JEWISH SAYING

THURSDAY
Easter
Week 4 _____

*[Jesus said after washing
the feet of his disciples,] "I have set
an example for you, so that you will do
just what I have done. . . . No messenger
is greater than the one who sent him."*

JOHN 13:15–16

Eastern Mennonite College placed
an unusual ad in *Campus Life* magazine.
After describing how everyone today
is striving to be "on top," the ad noted
that it was the same in Jesus' day.
Even his closest disciples wanted to be
"on top." In today's reading, Jesus makes
a dramatic statement about this attitude,
and he makes it in a dramatic way.
He ties a towel around his waist
and washes his disciples' feet.
In other words, he illustrates by example
what he had taught them by word:
Whoever wishes to be "on top"
should serve.
The ad concluded, "So if you want to be
the greatest, come and learn with us."

Why do I want to be "on top"?

*We will crawl under your car oftener
and get ourselves dirtier
than any of our competitors.*

SERVICE STATION SIGN

[Jesus said to his disciples,]
"I am going to prepare a place for you. . . .
[Then,] I will come back and take you
to myself, so that you will be where I am."

JOHN 14:2 3

After the bombing of Pearl Harbor
on December 7, 1941,
the Japanese invaded the Philippines.
Three months later, March 11, 1942,
General Douglas MacArthur
was forced to flee the Philippines.
Before leaving for Australia,
he told the islanders, "I shall return."
On October 20, 1944, he kept his promise.
Landing on Leyte Island,
MacArthur said, "I have returned."
Jesus, too, promised that after leaving
this world, he would someday return.
Like MacArthur, he will say,
"I have returned."

Do I long for Jesus' return
with the same ardor that the islanders
longed for MacArthur's return?

If the heart
is devoted to the mirage of the world,
to the creature instead of the Creator,
the disciple is lost.

DIETRICH BONHOEFFER

SATURDAY
Easter
Week 4 _____

[Jesus said,] "Believe me
when I say that I am in the Father
and the Father is in me. . . . Whoever
believes in me will do what I do—
yes, he will do even greater things,
because I am going to the Father."

JOHN 14:11-12

After filing his will,
Patrick Henry said, "I have now disposed
of all my property to my family.
There is one thing more
I wish I could give them,
and that is the Christian religion.
If they had that, and I had not given them
one shilling, they would have been rich,
and if they had not that,
and I had given them all the world,
they would be poor."
Jesus shows this same concern
for his disciples in today's reading.

What might I do if I seem to be failing,
at the present moment,
to pass on my faith to my loved ones?

We want to give our children
what we didn't have;
but let's make sure we give them
what we did have: our faith.

ANONYMOUS

[Jesus said,] "And now I give you
a new commandment: love one another.
As I have loved you,
so you must love one another.
If you have love for one another,
then everyone will know
that you are my disciples."

JOHN 13:34–35

Frederico Fellini's film *La Strada*
opened in 1954 and became a classic.
In one unforgettable scene,
a clown is talking to a young woman.
She has grown weary of trying to love
unlovable and unloving people, and
she wants nothing more to do with them.
As the conversation ends
and the young woman turns to leave,
the clown says to her,
"But if you don't love these people,
who will love them?"

The clown's words to the young woman
and Jesus' words to his disciples
invite me to inventory how ready I am
to take to heart what they say.

To love the world is no big chore.
It's that miserable person next door
who is the problem.

ANONYMOUS

MONDAY
Easter
Week 5 _____

[Jesus said,]
"Whoever accepts my commandments
and obeys them
is the one who loves me.
My father will love whoever loves me."

JOHN 14:21

Saint Augustine introduces
a beautiful passage in his writings
by asking, "What does love look like?"
He doesn't answer with metaphors
that compare love to a child's eyes
or to daisies dancing in the sunlight.
He answers in a more practical way:
"Love has hands to help others.
It has feet to hasten to the poor and needy.
It has eyes to see misery and want.
It has ears to hear the sighs and sorrows
of others. That's what love looks like."
Saint Augustine echoes and spells out
what Jesus says about love
in today's reading of his instruction
to his disciples.

When I apply the words of Jesus
and Saint Augustine to my everyday life,
what conclusion do I draw?

The same fence that shuts others out
shuts us in.

AUTHOR UNKNOWN

TUESDAY
Easter
Week 5

[Jesus said to his disciples,]
"Peace is what I leave with you;
it is my own peace that I give you. . . .
Do not be worried [or] . . . afraid."

JOHN 14:27

London was bombed often and
mercilessly during World War II.
One night
an old man was standing on a hill
overlooking the city.
As he gazed upon the fire and the smoke
rising from the city, he began to weep.
"Is there no hope at all?" he sobbed.
Just then a gust of wind cleared
the smoke enough for him to see the cross
atop the dome of Saint Paul's Church.
At that instant
a wave of hope swept over him.
He stopped worrying and being afraid,
because he knew by his faith in Jesus
that there was a far greater power
than evil at work in the world.

How do I regain my hope
when I grow fearful and depressed
at all the evil in our world?

Hope is putting faith to work
when doubting would be easier.

E. C. McKENZIE

WEDNESDAY
Easter
Week 5

[Jesus said,]
"I am the vine, and you are the branches.
Whoever remains in me, and I in him,
will bear much fruit;
for you can do nothing without me."

JOHN 15:5

Paul Claudel's play *The Satin Slipper*
opens with a shipwreck at sea.
The sole survivor is a missionary
who has tied himself to the mainmast.
Sensing death's approach, he begins
to pray in words like this: "Lord Jesus,
thank you for letting me die like this.
You know how during my life
I sometimes found your teaching hard.
And sometimes I battled your will,
not remaining fully united to you.
But now, by letting me die
helplessly bound to a cross of my own,
you have given me a sense
of closeness and unity with you."

If I could choose the way I would die,
what would I choose—and why?

As the voice of death whispers
"You must go from earth,"
let us hear the voice of Christ saying,
"You are coming to me!"

NORMAN McLEOD

Jesus said,
"I love you just as the Father loves me;
remain in my love."

JOHN 15:9

During World War II, a prisoner escaped
from a labor detail in Auschwitz,
a Nazi concentration camp in Poland.
To discourage such escapes,
the Nazis randomly picked ten prisoners
to be killed.
One was the father of a family.
As the guards marched the victims away
to be executed, a priest stepped from
the ranks of the other prisoners
and volunteered to take the man's place.
The Nazi officer in charge was stunned,
but he regained his composure and said,
"Accepted."
The priest's heroic act of love
for a fellow prisoner
is a faint reflection of Jesus' love for us
and of the Father's love for Jesus.

How open am I to whatever act of love
the Holy Spirit may be inviting me
to make?

Love is an outstretched finger
pointing to God.

ANONYMOUS

FRIDAY
Easter
Week 5 _____

[Jesus said,]
"Love one another, just as I love you."

Head football coach Gene Stallings
of the University of Alabama fainted
when doctors told him that his only son,
Johnny, was born with Down's syndrome.
That was thirty years ago.
Today, Stallings regards Johnny's birth
as one of the great gifts of his life.
Johnny has taught him what true love is.
Stallings says of his son,
"All his love is unconditional.
He doesn't keep score.
He's totally unselfish."
Stallings says if he could change fate
and start over with a normal child,
he wouldn't. "Johnny has been such a big
part of my life," he said. "I wouldn't
change a thing. I feel very blessed."

What have I learned about love
from some member of my family?

Making the decision to have a child—
it's momentous.
It is to decide forever
to have your heart
walk around outside your body.
ELIZABETH STONE

[Jesus said to his followers,]
"If the world hates you,
just remember that it has hated me first."

JOHN 15:18

Jesus uses the term *world* here
in the theological sense, that is,
as a "human society organizing itself
without God" (WILLIAM BARCLAY).
It is this world
that persecuted Jesus (JOHN 15:20).
It is this world that Jesus identified
in some way with Satan (JOHN 17:15).
It is this world
that Jesus defeated (JOHN 16:33).
It is this world
that we will also defeat
by our faith in Jesus (1 JOHN 5:4).

How have I experienced in the past—
or how am I experiencing right now—
the negative impact of the world
that Jesus speaks of in today's reading?
What influence has it had on me?

Don't be blinded by prejudice,
disheartened by the times. . . .
Don't let anything paralyze your mind,
tie your hands,
or defeat your spirit.

WALTER FAUNTROY

SUNDAY
Easter
Week 6 _____

[Speaking of his departure from earth,
Jesus said to his disciples,]
"Peace is what I leave with you;
it is my own peace that I give you."

JOHN 14:27

Albert Schweitzer gave up
a successful musical career in Europe
to become a missionary doctor in Africa.
One day someone asked him
what starting point he used
to introduce Jesus and Jesus' message
to the members of African tribes.
He replied:
"When I speak of the difference between
the restless and the peaceful heart,
the wildest of my savages
knows what is meant.
And when I portray Jesus
as he who brings peace with God
to the human heart, they comprehend."

How does Jesus bring peace
to my own restless heart?

I shall ever try
to drive all evil away from my heart
and keep my love in flower,
knowing that you have your seat
in the inmost shrine of my heart.

RABINDRANATH TAGORE

"The Helper will come—the Spirit. . . .
I will send him to you from the Father,
and he will speak about me.
And you, too, will speak about me."

JOHN 15:26-27

A tribal chief lay dying.
He summoned three of his people and said,
"I must select a successor.
Climb our holy mountain and return
with the most precious gift you can find."
The first brought back a huge gold nugget.
The second brought back a priceless gem.
The third returned empty-handed, saying,
"When I reached the mountaintop,
I saw on the other side a beautiful land,
where people could go for a better life."
The chief said, "You shall succeed me.
You've brought back the most precious gift
of all: a vision of a better tomorrow."

It is such a vision that we Christians
are called by Jesus to bring to our world.
How well am I doing this?

[Jesus said,]
"What I am telling you in the dark
you must repeat in broad daylight, and
what you have heard in private
you must announce from the housetops."

MATTHEW 10:27

TUESDAY
Easter
Week 6 _____

*[Jesus said,] "I am going to him
who sent me. . . . And now that I have told
you, your hearts are full of sadness.
But . . . it is better for you that I go away,
because if I do not go, the Helper
[Holy Spirit] will not come to you."*

JOHN 16:5-7

A young Hindu and a young Christian
were taking the same seminar
on Jesus' Sermon on the Mount.
Early on they became good friends.
One day the Hindu said to the Christian,
"I know how this sermon of Jesus'
affected Gandhi and influenced his life,
but I fear its teaching is too lofty
for ordinary people."
Near the end of the course, the Hindu
found the answer to his dilemma.
The ethic was indeed lofty,
but he had overlooked Jesus' promise
to send the Spirit,
who would not only guide the people
but also empower them to live by it.

How frequently do I turn to the Spirit
for guidance and power?

*Where the human spirit fails,
the Holy Spirit fills.*

ANONYMOUS

WEDNESDAY
Easter
Week 6

[Jesus said,]
"I have much more to tell you,
but now it would be too much for you. . . .
When, however, the Spirit comes . . .
he will lead you into all the truth."

JOHN 16.12-13

Some Nicaraguan students were
on a boat trip to the island of Utila,
just off the country's northern coast.
One student asked to steer the ship.
The captain agreed, saying, "Okay, just
keep the needle at 335 degrees north."
Two hours later they arrived at Utila;
the student was still steering.
How did the student steer the boat
to an island the youth had never seen
and couldn't see at the start of the trip?
By simply following directions!
The Spirit is like that.
The Spirit can guide us to an "island"
that we have never seen
and cannot see at the moment.

When was the last time I asked the Spirit
for special guidance in some situation?

We must not be content
to be cleansed from sin;
we must be filled with the Spirit.

JOHN FLETCHER

THURSDAY
Easter
Week 6 _____

[Before ascending to his Father,
Jesus said to his disciples,]
"The message about repentance
and the forgiveness of sins
must be preached to all nations."

LUKE 24:47

The first part of Richard Bach's novel
Jonathan Livingston Seagull ends
with a scene strikingly similar
to Jesus' ascension into heaven.
Two gulls come to take Jonathan "home."
When Jonathan hesitates,
he is told, "One school is finished, and
the time has come for another to begin."
Suddenly, Jonathan realizes that
it was, indeed, time for him "to go home."
So he takes a last look at everything
that had been his home for so long.
Then in a burst of magnificent glory,
he "rose with the two star-bright gulls"
and disappeared into the sky.

What school ended for the disciples
when Jesus ascended? What one began?
How is my situation today
like the disciples' after Jesus ascended?

Evangelization is one beggar telling another
where he found bread.

D. T. NILES

*[Jesus said,] "Now you are sad,
but I will see you again, and
your hearts will be filled with gladness."*

JOHN 16:22

Doris Lee McCoy's book *Megatraits:
Twelve Traits of Successful People*
contains an interview with Peter Coors,
president of the Adolph Coors Company.
Adolph entered the United States
as a stowaway with no passport,
no papers, no money.
He went on to found one of the most
prestigious companies in America.
When Ms. McCoy asked Peter
(Adolph's great-grandson) what his idea
of success was, he said, "First, when my
life is completed, success would be
standing in front of God and feeling that,
although I've made some mistakes,
I've always had God at the center
of my life." It's this kind of joy
that Jesus refers to in today's reading.

How do I understand Peter's statement,
"I've always had God at the center
of my life"? Is this true of my life?

*If God loved us as much as we love God,
where would we all be?*

ANONYMOUS

SATURDAY
Easter
Week 6 _____

[Jesus said,]
"The Father will give you
whatever you ask of him in my name.
Until now you have not
asked for anything in my name;
ask and you will receive."

JOHN 16:23-24

A cartoon portrayed a tiny insect
peering up at a monster insect.
After staring at the monster for a while,
the tiny insect said,
"And what kind of a bug are you?"
"I'm a praying mantis," the monster said.
"That's absurd!" said the tiny insect.
"Bugs don't pray!"
With that, the praying mantis
grabbed the tiny bug around the throat
and squeezed. The bug's eyes bulged,
and it screamed, "Lord, help me!"
Some people are like that tiny bug.
They ignore—even ridicule—prayer
until they get squeezed.
Then they scream, "Lord, help me!"

What motivates me to keep praying,
especially when God seems
not to answer—or even hear me?

God's delay is not God's denial.

AUTHOR UNKNOWN

[At the Last Supper,
Jesus prayed to his heavenly Father
for his disciples, saying,]
"I pray not only for them,
but also for those who believe in me
because of their message.
I pray that they may all be one."

JOHN 17:20-21

In its "Points to Ponder" section,
Reader's Digest
carried this moving story by Cy Fey.
An elderly man was weeping noticeably
while standing alone at Washington's
Vietnam Veterans Memorial.
Moved by the sight, a young man walked
over to the old man, put his hand on his
shoulder, and said, "One of yours, sir?"
The old man said softly,
"Not *one* of them, son! *All* of them!"
This same spirit moved Jesus to pray
not just for his disciples alone
but for all believers.

Do my prayers ever reflect a concern
for all people—not just my loved ones?

Without love and compassion for others,
our own apparent love for Christ
is fiction.

THOMAS MERTON

MONDAY
Easter
Week 7

*[Before praying over his disciples
at the Last Supper, Jesus said to them,]
"The world will make you suffer.
But be brave! I have defeated the world!"*

JOHN 16:33

The wall of a Chicago dentist
is adorned with a colorful scroll
bearing the title "I Can Take It Club."
It contains
the names of hundreds of kids—
written in their own handwriting.
They are kids who have taken the pledge
not to complain or whimper
while the dentist works on them.
The dentist says it's absolutely amazing
how signing that pledge
turns kids from "babies" into "soldiers."
The spirit behind the list
is akin to the spirit behind Jesus' words
in today's reading.
Its purpose is to call forth
the best in us.

How can I be more creative in calling
forth the best in myself and others?

*It's all right
to have butterflies in your stomach.
Just get them to fly in formation.*

DR. ROB GILBERT

[Jesus] looked up to heaven and said,
"Father, the hour has come.
Give glory to your Son,
so that the Son may give glory to you."

JOHN 17:1

Three preachers were discussing
the best posture to use while praying.
The first said, "I've tried them all,
and kneeling is still the best."
The second said, "That may be true,
but most Eastern mystics recommend
sitting cross-legged on the floor."
The third said, "I pray best with my eyes
raised to heaven."
An electrician, working nearby,
overheard them and said, "For what it's
worth, fellas, the best prayer
I ever prayed was hanging by one leg
from a telephone pole in a thunderstorm."

Do I experiment with my prayer posture?
For example, do I ever pray the "prayer
before meditation" or "prayer after
meditation" (Lord's Prayer) out loud?
Do I ever raise my eyes to heaven or
kneel momentarily before prayer?

Come, let us bow down and worship . . . ;
let us kneel before the LORD.

PSALM 95:6

WEDNESDAY
Easter
Week 7 _____

*[Toward the end of his life, Jesus prayed
to his Father for his disciples, saying,]
"While I was with them, I kept them
safe. . . . And now I am coming to you."*
JOHN 17:12-13

Graham Greene's novel
The Power and the Glory deals with
religious persecution in Mexico.
One of its characters is an old priest.
The constant tension of being hunted
by the police takes its toll on him.
He turns to alcohol
and fails to serve his people properly.
Eventually he is captured
and sentenced to be executed.
The morning of the execution
he wakes up filled with sorrow.
"Tears poured down his face;
he was not . . . . afraid of damnation. . . . .
He felt only an immense disappointment
because he had to go to God empty-handed."
In his own mind, at least, he had failed.
How different it was with Jesus!

What is one way I could better carry out
the everyday job God has given me?

*Faithfulness in little things
is a big thing.*
SAINT JOHN CHRYSOSTOM

[Jesus said,]
"I pray that they may all be one. Father!"
JOHN 17:21

There is a story
about a group of shipwrecked people
adrift in a long, narrow lifeboat.
The boat is so long that people in the front
think of themselves as the "front" people,
and those in the back
think of themselves as the "back" people.
One day the front of the boat
develops an uncontrollable leak.
A man in the back of the boat
says to the woman next to him,
"Thank God that leak is in the front.
If it were in the back, we'd be doomed!"
That story contains an important lesson
for all of us in our world.
We forget that we're all in the same boat.
A serious threat to one part of the world
is a serious threat to every part.

Why do I agree/disagree with these words
of John F. Kennedy: "If a free society
cannot help the many who are poor,
it cannot save the few who are rich"?

We must learn to live together
as brothers or perish together as fools.
MARTIN LUTHER KING, JR.

FRIDAY
Easter
Week 7 _____

[Three times Jesus asked Peter,]
"Do you love me?" [Three times Peter said,]
"You know that I love you."
[Three times Jesus commissioned Peter,]
"Take care of my sheep."

JOHN 21:17

The Israelites viewed God as a shepherd:
"The LORD is my shepherd" (PSALM 23:1).
They also viewed their leaders,
God's representatives, as shepherds.
Ezekiel condemns them as *bad* shepherds
and says God will replace them (34:23).
It is against this background
that we must interpret Jesus' words:
"I am the *good shepherd*" (JOHN 10:11).
It is against this background also
that we must interpret Jesus' words
to Peter in today's reading.
Jesus (about to ascend to heaven)
commissions Peter to succeed him
as the shepherd of the flock.

What might I say to one who finds it
hard to see beyond the faults of church
leaders to their divine commission?

Nothing here below is profane
for those who know how to see.
On the contrary, everything is sacred.

TEILHARD DE CHARDIN

*[After indicating how "Peter would
die and bring glory to God"* (JOHN 21:19),
Jesus said to him,] "Follow me!"

JOHN 21:22

Rome was under serious siege in 1849.
The great Italian patriot Garibaldi issued
a challenge to all young men, saying,
"I have nothing to offer you but
hunger and thirst, hardship and death;
but I call on all who love their country
to join me." The response was amazing.
It was this kind of challenge
that Jesus held out to his followers.
It was this kind of challenge
that Jesus repeated, especially, to Peter
in today's reading.
It is this same challenge that Jesus
holds out to us, personally, today.

What might Jesus say to me if I asked
him why I should accept his challenge?

*Far better it is to dare mighty things,
to win glorious triumphs
even though checkered by failure
than to rank with those poor spirits
who neither enjoy nor suffer much
because they live in the gray twilight
that knows neither victory nor defeat.*

THEODORE ROOSEVELT

SUNDAY

Pentecost _____

*[Jesus breathed on his disciples
and said,] "Receive the Holy Spirit."*
JOHN 20:22

Joseph Sittler was walking down
a street in a poor section of Paris.
He came upon a little girl
who was wearing worn-out shoes
and a dress that looked like
"a sewed-up flour sack. . . .
She swung along the avenue
with a flower stuck in her black hair
and the grace of a princess,
as if to say, 'Here is a little French girl,
and don't you forget it.'
There is a kind of *elan* in the French spirit
that we are all aware of.
But when we try to nail the word down,
we're in trouble."
GRAVITY & GRACE

Such an *elan*—only infinitely greater—
filled Jesus' disciples on Pentecost.
And this same *elan* can fill us today,
if we but open ourselves to it.

What keeps me from asking Jesus to
"breathe" on me and fill my human spirit,
anew, with the *elan* of the Holy Spirit?

The human spirit is the lamp of the LORD.
PROVERBS 20:27 (NRSV)

_____ SPECIAL NOTE

Starting today (Monday after Pentecost), the Lectionary readings vary from year to year. To determine the reflection exercise to use today,

- locate the current year,
- read across to the week and page,
- turn to them and begin.

This will put you in the right sequence for the rest of the year. (For example, if the year is 1995, begin with Week 9, page 225.)

Year	Week	Page
1994	8	218
1995	9	225
1996	8	218
1997	7	211
1998	9	225
1999	8	218
2000	10	232
2001	9	225
2002	7	211
2003	10	232
2004	9	225
2005	7	211
2006	9	225
2007	8	218
2008	6	204
2009	9	225
2010	8	218

SEASON OF ORDINARY TIME

SUNDAY (Lord's Baptism)
Ordinary Time
Week 1

While [Jesus] was praying,
heaven was opened,
and the Holy Spirit came down upon him
in bodily form like a dove.
And a voice came down from heaven,
"You are my own dear Son.
I am pleased with you."

LUKE 3:21-22

Henry Ford hired an efficiency expert
to evaluate his company.
The expert's final report was favorable,
except for one thing. He said,
"Every time I pass by the office
of the man at the end of the hall,
I see him staring out the window
with his feet on the desk.
He's wasting your money."
"That man," said Henry, "had an idea once
that saved us millions of dollars.
At the time, I believe his feet
were planted right where they are now."

The image of the man lost in meditation
and the image of Jesus lost in prayer
make me ask, Would I be better off
if I made it a habit to pause occasionally
during my day to pray?

Life is fragile—handle with prayer.
E. C. McKENZIE

MONDAY
Ordinary Time
Week 1 _____

[Jesus] reflects
the brightness of God's glory and
is the exact likeness of God's own being.
HEBREWS 1:3

Saint Ambrose
was a fourth-century bishop of Milan.
His preaching played a major role
in Saint Augustine's conversion.
In one of his homilies,
Ambrose used the following example
to illusrate how Jesus mirrors God:
"As the print of the seal on the wax
is the express image of the seal itself,
so Christ is the express image—
the perfect representation—of God."
It is this image
that today's reading sets before us.
Jesus' love mirrors God's love.
Jesus' mercy mirrors God's mercy.
Jesus' gentleness
mirrors God's gentleness.

What is one practical way
I could become a better mirror of Jesus
in my own daily life?

Anyone who has really understood
that God became human can never
speak and act in an inhuman way.
KARL BARTH

*For a little while [Jesus]
was made lower than the angels,
so that through God's grace
he should die for everyone.
We see him now
crowned with glory and honor.*

HEBREWS 2:9

Jesus breaks all conventional molds.
He praises pagans and prostitutes
(LUKE 7:9, 36–50).
He relates to Samaritans and lepers
(LUKE 10:33–37, 17:11–18).
He attacks leaders (MATTHEW 23:3),
welcomes children (MATTHEW 19:14),
calms storms (MARK 4:39), and
falls silent before his accusers
(MATTHEW 27:13–14).
No one would have written
such a scenario for a religious leader.
"Precisely for this reason
the Gospels have undying power
to convert humble hearts."

AVERY DULLES

What is a humble heart,
and how might I develop one?

*[Jesus said,] "Learn from me, because
I am gentle and humble in spirit."*

MATTHEW 11:29

WEDNESDAY
Ordinary Time
Week 1 _____

[Jesus] can help those who are tempted,
because he himself was tempted.

HEBREWS 2:18

Frederic Remington
was an American sculptor
who worked in the early 1900s.
His artistic creations sell today
for as much as $100,000.
One his famous works, *The Rattlesnake,*
depicts a horse and horseman
encountering a snake on a path.
The horse
is reared up on its two hind legs,
the horseman is holding on mightily,
and the rattlesnake is poised to strike.
This brilliant sculpture
acts as a parable of how we should react
when we encounter temptation.
We should react as quickly and seriously
as did the horse and the horseman.

Do I really believe
Jesus can help me when I am tempted?
How do I explain the times
when I asked Jesus' help
but gave into the temptation anyway?

We are not tempted because we are evil;
we are tempted because we are human.

FULTON J. SHEEN (slightly adapted)

We are all partners with Christ
if we hold firmly to the end
the confidence we had at the beginning.

HEBREWS 3:14

During his second year
with the Cleveland Indians,
23-year-old Herb Score won 20 games
and led both leagues in strikeouts.
Then came the night of May 7, 1958.
Pitching against the Yankees,
he was hit in the face by a line drive.
Herb hit the ground with a thud.
Blood streamed from his right eye.
He said later, "I was afraid I was blind,
and I prayed to God."
Eventually Herb's sight returned,
but his brilliant career ended that night.
Nevertheless, he picked up the pieces
and carried on as a sportscaster.

Where do I find strength
to pick up the pieces and begin again?

When everything goes against you,
till it seems as though
you could not hold on a minute longer,
never give up then,
for that is just the place and time
that the tide will turn.

HARRIET BEECHER STOWE

FRIDAY
Ordinary Time
Week 1 _____

*God has offered us the promise
that we may receive that rest
he spoke about. . . . Let us, then,
do our best to receive that rest.*

HEBREWS 4:1, 11

A frustrated mother asked her little boy,
"How do you expect to get into heaven?"
He thought a minute and said,
"Well, I'll run in and out, and in and out,
and keep slamming the door.
Then an angel will say,
'For heaven's sake, stay in or stay out!'
Then, I'll stay in!"
The mother was trying to do for her son
what the author of Hebrews
was trying to do for his readers:
make them aware
that entering God's rest (heaven)
is the most important concern
that should be on our mind during life.
It is for this that we were made.

How well does my life reflect the fact
that my ultimate destiny
is not to remain on earth
but to go to heaven?

*Everyone wants to go to heaven,
but nobody wants to die.*

JOE LOUIS, former heavyweight champ

*We have a great High Priest
who has gone into the very presence
of God—Jesus, the Son of God.
Our High Priest is not one who cannot
feel sympathy for our weaknesses.
On the contrary, we have a High Priest
who was tempted in every way
that we are, but did not sin.*

HEBREWS 4:14–15

In 1982 Archbishop Glemp of Warsaw
urged Polish young people
not to grow discouraged or frustrated
in their efforts to bring about change.
He told them he sympathized with them
because he himself was beaten by police
in his youth for pressing for change.
Likewise his father was punished for
pressing for change against the Nazis.
As Archbishop Glemp understood
the frustrations of Polish youth,
so Jesus understands our frustrations,
for he was like us in all things but sin.

What is one frustration
I am currently suffering?
How can Jesus help me deal with it?

*Few happinesses equal the joy
of finding a heart that understands.*
VICTOR ROBINSOLL (slightly adapted)

174

There was a wedding in the town of Cana
in Galilee. Jesus' mother was there. . . .
When the wine had given out,
Jesus' mother . . . told the servants,
"Do whatever [Jesus] tells you." . . .
Jesus said to the servants,
"Fill these jars with water."
[They did, and the water turned to wine.]

JOHN 2:1, 3-5, 7

After college,
University of Michigan quarterback and
Heisman Trophy winner Tom Harmon
became a pilot. One day his plane crashed
deep in a South American jungle.
Miraculously, he survived.
Describing his experience, he wrote,
"I said at least a million 'Hail Marys'
during my trek out.
In fact, as I walked through the jungle,
trying to find my way out, I used to yell
'Hail Marys' at the top of my voice,
hoping that someone would hear me and
at the same time I would be praying."

How important a role does Mary,
Jesus' mother, play in my spiritual life?

God could not be everywhere,
so he made mothers.

JEWISH PROVERB

[Jesus] learned through his sufferings
to be obedient.
When he was made perfect, he became
the source of eternal salvation
for all those who obey him.

HEBREWS 5:8-9

A little boy hated stewed prunes.
Yet he managed to eat all but two.
His mother insisted that he eat them also.
He refused, so she sent him to bed, saying,
"God can't stand disobedient boys;
he gets very, very angry at them!"
That night a violent storm blew up.
Lightning flashed and thunder crashed.
The mother feared that her son
would be frightened to death.
So she went to his room to comfort him.
She found him at the window,
staring out into the storm and saying,
"All that fuss over two prunes!"

What is my main motive
for obeying God's law—fear or love?
How strong is that motive?

I'll go where you want me to go, dear Lord,
O'er mountain or plain or sea;
I'll say want you want me to say, dear Lord,
I'll be what you want me to be.

MARY BROWN

TUESDAY
Ordinary Time
Week 2 _____

*[God] will not forget the work you did
or the love you showed for him
in the help you gave and are still giving
to your fellow Christians.*

HEBREWS 6:10

A doctor used to prescribe
"memory breaks" for hospital patients.
Before leaving a room, he would say,
"I have one more prescription for you.
I want you to take a memory break:
one at ten o'clock and another at four.
Here's what you do.
Close your eyes and recall a happy time
from your past.
Spend as much time as you can
recalling and reliving it."
The doctor knew what he was doing.
Memory breaks are healing experiences.
Today's Bible reading assures us
that someday God will take
a similar memory break with us.
God will recall the good we did on earth.
That will be a great healing experience.

What memory, especially,
will God recall for me at that time?

*God gives us memory
so that we can have roses in December.*
JAMES MATTHEW BARRIE

Melchizedek was . . . a priest
of the Most High God. As Abraham
was coming back from the battle
in which he defeated the four kings,
Melchizedek met him and blessed him,
and Abraham gave him
one tenth of all he had taken.

HEBREWS 7:1-2

Bishop Harry Flynn of Lafayette,
Louisiana, was visiting a prison.
As he was leaving,
a prisoner asked him for a rosary.
The bishop had in his pocket
a Connemara marble rosary from Ireland.
Although he hated to part with it,
he gave it to the prisoner.
When the bishop got home, someone
was waiting there with a gift for him.
When the bishop saw the gift,
he couldn't believe his eyes.
It was a rosary identical to the one
that he had given the prisoner.

When was the last time
I was especially generous
with my time, money, or belongings?

Give to the world the best you have
and the best will come back to you.

ANONYMOUS

THURSDAY
Ordinary Time
Week 2 _____

[Jesus] is able,
now and always, to save those
who come to God through him,
because he lives forever
to plead with God for them.

HEBREWS 7:25

At one point during World War II,
German planes bombed London nightly.
People lost homes and businesses
at the drop of a bomb.
People also suffered countless
bodily injuries, many of which
doctors were too busy to treat.
An elderly woman, a Mrs. Berwick,
bought a first-aid kit.
Then she printed a sign and hung it
on the door of her house. It read,
"If you need help, knock here!"
William Barclay uses this moving story
to illustrate
that Jesus is always ready to help us
in a similar way.
All we have to do is "knock."

How might I deepen my personal faith
in Jesus' readiness to help me?

"The door will be opened
to anyone who knocks."

LUKE 11:10

FRIDAY
Ordinary Time
Week 2

[The Lord says,]
"I will forgive their sins and
will no longer remember their wrongs."

HEBREWS 8:12

In an article in *TV Guide,*
Jane Fonda describes
her movie-star father, Henry,
as being a "shy,
somewhat troubled and distant parent"
who "didn't know
how to reach out" to his children.
She goes on to say
that now that she has experienced
being a parent, she realizes
that "blame and judgment
are no way to go through life.
Forgiveness is important.
You can't grow up until you can forgive,
and it's the child
who must usually make the first move."

To what extent do I make the first move
in repairing fractured relationships—
especially with older family members?

If you have anything to pardon,
pardon quickly.
Slow forgiveness is little better
than no forgiveness.

SIR ARTHUR PINERO

SATURDAY
Ordinary Time
Week 2 _____

*[Christ] did not take
the blood of goats and bulls
to offer as a sacrifice;
rather, he took his own blood.*

HEBREWS 9:12

Lieutenant Richard Pembrey
was a surgeon
in the British armed forces
during World War II.
In his book *The Sands of Dunkirk,*
he tells how he witnessed
an act of sacrifice that made him weep.
A soldier, realizing he was dying,
took the only blanket
covering him in his final hours
and placed it over the shivering body
of a pneumonia-stricken soldier
in the next bunk.

The soldier's sacrifice in his last hours
and Jesus' sacrifice on the cross invite
me to ask about my spirit of sacrifice.
When did I last make a great sacrifice?

*One secret act of self-denial,
one sacrifice of inclination to duty,
is worth all the mere good thoughts,
warm feelings, passionate prayers
in which idle people indulge themselves.*

JOHN HENRY NEWMAN

SUNDAY
Ordinary Time
Week 3

On the Sabbath
[Jesus] went as usual to the synagogue.
He stood up to read the Scriptures . . .
where it is written,
"The Spirit of the Lord is upon me,
because he has chosen me
to bring good news to the poor.
He has sent me to proclaim liberty
to the captives and recovery of sight
to the blind, to set free the oppressed
and announce that the time has come
when the Lord will save his people."

LUKE 4:16–19

U.S. presidents give an inaugural speech
right after being sworn into office.
The speech usually provides an insight
into what to expect from them.
Today's gospel is like such a speech.
Jesus has been chosen by the Father
for the office of Messiah.
Jesus begins by standing up in public
and telling us what to expect from him
during his messianic ministry.

What surprises me most/least about
what Jesus says in his inaugural? Why?

I know men, and I tell you
that Jesus Christ is not a man.
NAPOLEON BONAPARTE

MONDAY
Ordinary Time
Week 3 —————————————————————

[Christ] has appeared once and for all,
to remove sin
through the sacrifice of himself.

HEBREWS 9:26

The singing career
of Grammy award winner Marvin Gaye
ended abruptly in the 1980s,
when his own father shot and killed him.
The singer's childhood was tormented
by cruelty inflicted upon him
by his father.
This cruelty left a wound in Marvin
that never healed.
Referring to this tragic situation,
the singer's close friend and biographer,
David Ritz, wrote,
"Marvin really believed in Jesus a lot,
but he could never apply the teaching
of Jesus on forgiveness
to his own father.
In the end it destroyed them both."

Marvin's failure to follow the example
of Jesus and forgive invites me to recall
someone who hurt me and to ask Jesus
to help me forgive him or her fully.

The narrow soul
knows not the glory of forgiveness.

FREDERICK W. ROBERTSON

When Christ was about to come
into the world, he said . . .
"Here I am, to do your will, O God."

HEBREWS 10:5, 7

Someone asked a famous conductor
of a symphony orchestra
what instrument was hardest to play.
Without hesitation, he replied,
"Second fiddle!
I can get plenty of first violins,
but I can find very few musicians
who are willing to play second fiddle,
especially with enthusiasm.
And that's the problem.
No second-fiddle player; no harmony.
It's as simple as all that."

Jesus' words about coming to do
God's will and the conductor's words
about the difficulty of finding someone
to play "second fiddle" invite me
to inventory my enthusiasm
for doing God's will,
even if it calls for playing "second fiddle."

No service in itself is small,
None great though earth it fill;
But that is small that seeks its own,
And great that seeks God's will.

ANONYMOUS

WEDNESDAY
Ordinary Time
Week 3 _____

*[The Lord] says, "I will not remember
their sins and evil deeds any longer."*
HEBREWS 10:17

In *Forgive and Forget,*
Lewis Smedes tells about a prisoner
who worked in a Nazi field hospital.
One day a nurse escorted him
to the bed of a dying German soldier.
The soldier asked to be forgiven
for his part in the Holocaust, saying,
"I know what I am asking
is almost too much,
but without your forgiveness
I cannot die in peace."
The prisoner thought a long minute
and then walked away,
without forgiving the soldier.
The prisoner survived the war
but could not forget the incident.
It bothered him the rest of his life.

What would I recommend to someone
who finds it hard to forgive another?
Why this?

*When we cannot forgive, we break
the bridge over which we must pass
if we would ever reach heaven;
for everyone has need to be forgiven.*
GEORGE HERBERT (adapted)

Let us be concerned for one another,
to help one another to show love
and to do good.

HEBREWS 10:24

Ted Kennedy, Jr.,
lost his leg to cancer at the age of 12.
In his 20s he spent a lot of time
giving inspirational talks
to others in his situation.
Of his recovery he says:
"People give me too much credit.
So much of it was that my family . . .
could afford
the best doctors and best treatment.
One of the reasons
I'm getting involved in speaking is
that I want to repay some of that debt.
It takes so little for me
to make others feel better
that it would be unthinkable
not to make the effort."

How can I thank God and my family for
the blessings they've showered on me?

Happiness will never be ours
if we do not recognize to some degree
that God's blessings were given us
for the well-being of all.

ANONYMOUS

FRIDAY
Ordinary Time
Week 3 _____

Do not lose your courage . . .
because it brings with it a great reward.
You need to be patient,
in order to do the will of God
and receive what he promises.

HEBREWS 10:35-36

The movie *Running Brave*
tells the story of Billy Mills, who rose
from poverty on an Indian reservation
to win a gold medal
in the Tokyo Olympics in 1964.
Billy's victory came the hard way.
He had to run in borrowed shoes,
labor under the false charge
that he was a quitter,
and battle back after being bumped
off the track by a competitor.
Billy showed
the kind of courage and patience
that today's Bible reading talks about.

Can I recall a time when I had to reach
down into myself for the kind of virtue
that today's reading describes?
What role does God play in such virtue?

Hold on with a bulldog grip, and chew
and choke as much as possible.

PRESIDENT LINCOLN to General Grant
during the siege of Petersburg

*It was faith that made Abraham able
to become a father,
even though he was too old and
Sarah herself could not have children.
He trusted God to keep his promise.*

HEBREWS 11:11

On a cellar wall in Cologne, Germany,
an unknown World War II fugitive
from the Nazis
left a beautiful testimony of faith.
Workers found the inscription
while clearing away debris
from a bombed-out house. It read:
"I believe in the sun
even when it is not shining.
I believe in love
even when I do not feel it.
I believe in God
even when he is silent."

The fugitive's faith and Abraham's faith
invite me to speak to God
about my faith. What do I say?

*Take clay and dust, and fashion a child/
With wistful brown eyes and breath
in its lungs;/ Make flesh-warm lips,
a brain, and red blood—/ Then, if you
succeed, tell me there's no God.*

CARRIE ESTHER HAMMILL

SUNDAY
Ordinary Time
Week 4 _____

[Jesus claimed that Isaiah's prophecy
about the Messiah applied to him.]
When the people
in the synagogue [at Nazareth]
heard this, they were filled with anger
[and rejected Jesus violently].

LUKE 4:28

Jesus' rejection
by the people of his hometown
previews what will take place often
in the days ahead:
people will reject Jesus—even violently.
Today, people
still reject Jesus and his teaching.
When asked why he didn't follow Jesus,
a high school boy said bluntly,
"Because if I did,
many of my friends would reject me—
just as many of Jesus' friends
rejected him.
And I couldn't take
that kind of rejection right now."

How much has peer pressure influenced
my following of Jesus in the past?
How much is it influencing it right now?

We forfeit three-fourths of ourselves
to be like other people.

ARTHUR SCHOPENHAUER

*There isn't enough time for me to speak
of Gideon, Barak, Samson, Jephthah,
David, Samuel, and the prophets.
Through faith
they fought whole countries and won.
They did what was right
and received what God had promised.*

HEBREWS 11:32-33

Concert musician Itzhak Perlman says
two things happened before he was four
to shape his future:
He was struck with polio,
and he heard Jascha Heifetz play.
The polio took away his legs,
but the music of Heifetz gave him wings.
It gave him a dream
that inspired him to pursue greatness.
Perlman is a faint, modern reflection
of the great biblical heroes.
These heroes also suffered much,
but they also had a dream
that inspired them to pursue greatness.

What dream inspires me to keep going,
even in times of suffering and trial?

*What we suffer at this present time
cannot be compared at all with the glory
that is going to be revealed to us.*

ROMANS 8:18

TUESDAY
Ordinary Time
Week 4 _____

Let us keep our eyes fixed on Jesus. . . .
He did not give up because
of the cross! . . . So do not let yourselves
become discouraged and give up.

HEBREWS 12:2-3

There's a dance in the movie *Funny Face*
in which Fred Astaire
knocks a top hat off his head with a cane
and catches it on his heel.
That trick looks so easy on the screen.
But it took 30 tries before the camera.
When Astaire
picked up his hat the 29th time,
we can imagine the film director saying,
"Let's give up that idea!"
But Astaire wasn't made that way.
Nothing could make him
give up on an idea
if he thought it was worth doing.

What keeps me going
in times of trial and discouragement?
Speak to Jesus about what kept him
going in such times.

Many people have thrown up their hands
at a time when a little more effort
and a little more patience
would have achieved success.

ELBERT HUBBARD (slightly adapted)

_____ SPECIAL NOTE

Starting with Wednesday of the fourth week of Ordinary time, the Lectionary readings vary from year to year, depending on when Ash Wednesday (start of Lent) falls in that year.

The following table shows the date on which Ash Wednesday falls in the years ahead. Locate the current year and, on the date indicated, turn to page 67 (Ash Wednesday) and begin there.

1994	February 16
1995	March 1
1996	February 21
1997	February 12
1998	February 25
1999	February 17
2000	March 8
2001	February 28
2002	February 13
2003	March 5
2004	February 25
2005	February 9
2006	March 1
2007	February 21
2008	February 6
2009	February 25
2010	February 17

WEDNESDAY
Ordinary Time
Week 4 _____

Lift up your tired hands . . .
and strengthen your trembling knees! . . .
Guard against turning back
from the grace of God.

HEBREWS 12:12, 15

A boy was working in a London store.
Each morning he'd rise at five o'clock
and then work a 14-hour day.
For two years this went on.
He became deeply depressed
and thought of suicide.
One day he wrote a pathetic letter
to a former teacher and described
how he no longer wanted to live.
The teacher wrote him
a deeply personal letter in return.
It was filled with encouragement,
genuine affirmation, and real love.
That letter changed the boy's life.
Eventually, he became one of England's
best-known writers, H. G. Wells.

When did I last sacrifice time or effort
to help someone like the boy? Who is
someone who might need my help now?

Our chief want in life
is somebody who shall make us do
what we can.

RALPH WALDO EMERSON

The people of Israel came . . .
to Mount Sinai with its blazing fire,
the darkness and the gloom,
the storm, the blast of a trumpet. . . .
The sight was so terrifying
that Moses said,
"I am trembling and afraid!"

HEBREWS 12:18–19, 21

A woman said,
"I always had a problem
reconciling biblical passages that said
'fear of God' was the start of wisdom
and passages that said 'God is love.'
Then one day I read something
that helped me immensely.
It was this line from Rod McKuen:
'I love the sea
But it doesn't make me less afraid of it.' "

What is Rod McKuen's point,
and how does it give me an insight
into how love and fear can coexist
when it comes to my relationship
with God?

Long to see God,
fear losing God, and
find joy in whatever leads to God.
Do this, and you'll find great peace.

SAINT TERESA OF AVILA

FRIDAY
Ordinary Time
Week 4 _____

Keep on loving one another. . . .
Remember those who are suffering,
as though you were suffering
as they are.

HEBREWS 13:1, 3

Patt Blue, a *Life* magazine photographer,
was on an extended assignment
in a hospital.
There she made the acquaintance
of Carrie, a victim of multiple sclerosis.
In her journal for September 17, 1979,
Patt writes:
"The nurses aides or whatever they are
seem to hate their jobs—
they sit and watch TV. . . .
When Carrie is put in a wheelchair,
no one talks to her like a human being.
She falls over—no attempt is made
to straighten her out."

The neglect of Carrie by the nurses aides
and the word of God in today's reading
invite me to ask,
How attentive am I to the needs of those
assigned to my care?

Of all earthly music
that reaches farthest into heaven
is the beating of a truly loving heart.

HENRY WARD BEECHER

May the God of peace . . . ,
through Jesus Christ,
do in us what pleases him.
HEBREWS 13:21

Shortly after Mikhail Baryshnikov
defected from the Soviet Union,
he performed at the Kennedy Center
for two weeks. A critic wrote:
"As the two weeks went by
I realized something
more amazing than the dancing. . . .
A young woman, Gelsey Kirkland, . . .
had been chosen by Baryshnikov
to be his partner. . . .
She sparkled; she was radiant;
she was full of life.
And I realized that I was seeing
the miracle of one person bringing out
in another person her very best."
God wants to work this same miracle
in us through God's Son, Jesus.

What is there in Jesus that brings out
the sparkle and the very best in me?

God be thanked
for that good and perfect gift . . .
His life, His love,
His very self in Jesus Christ.
MALBIE BABCOCK

SUNDAY
Ordinary Time
Week 5 —————————————

[Peter, James, and John]
pulled the boats up on the beach,
left everything, and followed Jesus.
LUKE 5:11

Tony de Mello, an Indian priest,
did a satellite television program
that was beamed to 76 universities
in the United States and Canada
and involved 3,000 students in dialogue.
Tony grew up near Bombay, India.
One day he came home from high school
and asked his father
if he could become a Catholic priest.
His father said, "No, you're my only son.
I want you to carry on the family name."
Then, after being childless for 14 years,
Tony's mother became pregnant.
When she was later rushed to the hospital
for delivery,
Tony ran the four-mile distance on foot.
Arriving out of breath,
he asked his dad, "Is it a boy or a girl?"
"You have a brother," his dad said.
"Great!" said Tony. "Now I can be a priest."

How enthusiastically do I follow Jesus?
Where does my enthusiasm come from?

Enthusiasm begets heroism.
S. M. DUBNOV

MONDAY
Ordinary Time
Week 5

In the beginning . . .
God created the universe. . . .
The earth produced all kinds of plants,
and God was pleased with what he saw.

GENESIS 1:1, 12

Jacques Cousteau used to take
his young son, Jean-Michel, with him
on his undersea explorations.
Jean-Michel said later,
"My father imparted to me the belief
that we are not the owners of the
world's resources, but its stewards . . .
responsible for protecting what we have
for those who will follow. . . .
But as I travel
I am struck by how infrequently
we keep future generations in mind."

How am I trying to exercise responsible
stewardship of the earth's resources?

The earth belongs as much
to those who are to come after us . . .
as to us;
and we have no right,
by anything we do or neglect,
to involve them
in unnecessary penalties, or
deprive them of benefits.

JOHN RUSKIN

TUESDAY
Ordinary Time
Week 5 _____

God commanded, "Let the water be filled
with many kinds of living beings. . . ."
And God was pleased. . . . Then God . . .
created human beings . . . and said . . .
"I am putting you in charge of the fish,
the birds, and all the wild animals."

GENESIS 1:20, 21, 26-28

Marion Stoddard spearheaded
a drive in Groton, Massachusetts,
to clean up the Nashua River.
It was so polluted people joked it was
"too thick to pour and too thin to plow."
About the success of the drive, she said,
"You don't have to be real smart;
you just have to identify the people
with power, the people who care,
and be committed, persistent and honest."
Stanley Jones
launched a similar drive to clean up
the Kankakee River in Kankakee, Illinois.
"Show people that somebody cares,"
said Jones, "and all apathy disappears."

On a scale of one (not very) to ten (very),
how caring am I about the kind of planet
we will be passing on to our children?
How is my care translating into action?

Let's not make God a slumlord.
ROBERT ORBEN

Then the LORD God
took some soil from the ground
and formed a man out of it;
he breathed life-giving breath into his
nostrils and the man began to live. . . .
Then the LORD God placed the man
in the Garden of Eden
to cultivate it and guard it.

GENESIS 2:7, 15

A cartoon strip of "Calvin and Hobbes"
shows Hobbes frustrated
at how people are treating our planet.
He turns to Calvin and says,
"One reason
why I think there's intelligent life
on other planets is that
they are avoiding contact with us."

How do I feel about these words
attributed to Chief Seattle: "The rivers
are our brothers; they quench our thirst.
The rivers carry our canoes
and feed our children. . . .
Teach your children
that the rivers are our brothers . . .
and give the rivers the kindness
you would give any brother"?

Nature is God's living, visible garment.
JOHANN WOLFGANG VON GOETHE

THURSDAY
Ordinary Time
Week 5 _____

Then the LORD God
made the man fall into a deep sleep,
and while he was sleeping,
he took out one of the man's ribs
and closed up the flesh.
He formed a woman out of the rib
and brought her to him. . . .
That is why a man leaves his father and
mother and is united with his wife,
and they become one.

GENESIS 2:21-22, 24

Reflecting on the biblical imagery
of the origin of woman,
Gordon Higham wrote this meditation:
"Woman was taken
not from man's head to be ruled by him,
nor from his feet to be trampled upon,
but from his side to walk beside him,
from under his arm
to be protected by him,
and from near his heart
to be loved by him."

What is one positive and loving way
that my attitude toward my spouse
has changed over the years?

The best thing a father can do for
his children is to love their mother.

THEODORE HESBURG

*[The snake told Adam and Eve to eat
the fruit, saying,] "You will be like God
and know what is good and what is bad."
. . . As soon as they had eaten it,
they were given understanding
and realized that they were naked
[and they hid from God].*

GENESIS 3:4, 7

God's dealings with us
might be compared to a three-act play:
Act 1—Creation (God creates us),
Act 2—De-creation (we sin),
Act 3—Re-creation (God saves us).
Act 1 ends with the making
of the first woman.
Act 2 begins with the commission
of the first sin.
Act 3 begins with God saying to Satan
concerning the woman,
"Her offspring [ultimately Jesus]
will crush your head" (GENESIS 3:15).

How vividly can I recall the beginning
of those same three "acts" in my life?

*True repentance hates the sin,
and not merely the penalty;
and it hates the sin most of all because
it has discovered and felt God's love.*

WILLIAM M. TAYLOR

SATURDAY
Ordinary Time
Week 5 _____

[God said to the man,]
"Because of what you have done,
the ground will be under a curse. . . .
You will have to work hard . . .
to make the soil produce anything,
until you go back to the soil
from which you were formed."

GENESIS 3:17, 19

In his novel *Studs Lonigan*,
James Farrell has someone cry out,
"God, why do you not raise
one little finger to save man from . . .
suffering on this planet?"
Ancient peoples also cried out
about all the suffering on the planet.
They asked their holy people,
"If we human beings are responsible
for *moral* evil (sin), who is responsible
for *physical* evil (suffering)?"
The Bible answers this question
in today's reading.
Suffering is not the result of a defect
in God's creation, but our misuse of it.

How might I be adding to human suffering,
right now, by my sins?

We are not punished for our sins,
but by them.

ELBERT HUBBARD (slightly adapted)

[Jesus said,]
"Happy are you who are hungry now;
you will be filled!"

LUKE 6:21

Time's cover story (May 10, 1993)
dealt with Hillary Rodham Clinton.
It described the First Lady's speech
given at the University of Texas
on the day before her father died.
Her voice broke as she quoted
Lee Atwater (Bush campaign manager),
who died at age 40 of a brain tumor.
He had acquired wealth and honor,
but felt a deep inner emptiness, saying,
"My illness helped me to see
that what was missing in society
is what is missing in me—
a little heart, a lot of brotherhood."
He concluded, "We must . . .
speak to this spiritual vacuum
at the heart of American society."

How well can I relate to Lee Atwater's
remarks? What can just one person do
when it comes to speaking to the
spiritual vacuum in American society?

Who loseth wealth loseth much . . .
but who loseth the spirit loseth all.
ELBERT HUBBARD (slightly adapted)

MONDAY
Ordinary Time
Week 6

*[The LORD banished Cain for killing
his brother Abel. Cain lamented,]
"I will be a homeless wanderer . . . and
anyone who finds me will kill me." . . .
So the LORD put a mark on Cain
to warn anyone who met him
not to kill him.*

GENESIS 4:14-15

Ancient owners marked their slaves
with tattoos or brands.
The mark identified the slave
as belonging to them.
It also protected the slave.
A person would think twice before
harming the slave of a powerful owner.
This background
helps us understand the point
of today's Scripture reading.
The mark put on Cain identifies him
as belonging to the LORD.
It is also a kind of merciful protection.

How is my own personal story
somewhat similar to
the personal story of Cain?

*Let no one give me any more trouble,
because the scars I have on my body
show that I am the slave of Jesus.*

GALATIANS 6:17

*When the LORD saw
how wicked everyone on earth was
and how evil
their thoughts were all the time,
he was sorry that he had ever made them
and put them on earth.*

GENESIS 6.5-6

James Huberty took a gun and
drove to a fast-food restaurant
in San Ysidro, California.
Minutes later,
21 people lay dead and 19 lay injured.
Sometime later, on KFMB-TV,
Huberty's wife said her husband got up,
dressed, and headed for the door.
"Where are you going, honey?" she asked.
"I'm going to hunt humans," he replied.
This kind of madness
helps us appreciate the point
of today's Scripture reading.

What can I do
about the madness of sin in the world?
About the madness of sin in my life?

*We'll never stop crime
until we get over the idea
that we can hire or elect people
to stop it.*

ANONYMOUS

WEDNESDAY
Ordinary Time
Week 6 _____

*[After the flood, the ark came to rest
on a mountain in the Ararat range.]
Noah built an altar to the LORD. . . .
The odor of the sacrifice
pleased the LORD.*

GENESIS 8:20-21

Biblical fundamentalists
have sponsored dozens of expeditions
to search for Noah's ark.
In 1955 they found an L-shaped beam
13,500 feet up the mountain range.
Using the carbon-14 dating process,
scientists dated it back to A.D. 700.
Scholars speculate the beam
came from a shrine built by early monks
in imitation of the biblical ark.
Most scholars hold that the flood story
belongs to biblical *prehistory* and
should be interpreted as a *symbol* story.
Its purpose is to teach that sin
leads people down a dead-end street.
It ends in the senseless destruction
of ourselves and of our world.
God alone can save us.

How keen is my personal sense of sin?

*Our sense of sin
is in proportion to our nearness to God.*

THOMAS D. BRAINARD

[God promised Noah and his sons,]
"Never again will all living beings
be destroyed by a flood; never again
will a flood destroy the earth."

GENESIS 9:11

Clarence Day's autobiographical work
Life with Father
had one of the longest runs
of any American play in history.
Clarence Day also authored
another autobiographical work
called *God and My Father.*
In it he writes:
"Father expected a good deal of God.
He didn't actually
accuse God of inefficiency,
but when he prayed
his tone was loud and angry,
like that of a dissatisfied guest
in a carelessly managed hotel."

To what extent do I tend to blame God
for not arresting the tide of evil
that threatens to destroy our world?

Racism is yours, end it.
Injustice is yours, correct it. . . .
Ignorance is yours, banish it.
War is yours, stop it.

WALTER FAUNTROY

FRIDAY
Ordinary Time
Week 6 _____

[Noah's descendants said to one another,]
"Now let's build a city
with a tower that reaches the sky, so
that we can make a name for ourselves."

GENESIS 11:4

The musical sounds coming from a radio
are dependent upon the radio.
When the radio goes on, the sounds go on.
When the radio goes off, they go off.
Suppose, one day, they said to the radio,
"We declare our independence from you.
From now on, we will decide
whether we go on or go off.
We don't need you any longer."
Such a situation would be ludicrous.
Yet today's Bible reading
presents a situation somewhat like this.
Noah's descendants are portrayed
as declaring independence from God,
who made them and holds them in being.

In what way, perhaps, do I tend
to declare my independence from God?

Sin has four characteristics:
self-sufficiency instead of faith,
self-will instead of submission,
self-seeking instead of benevolence,
self-righteousness instead of pride.

E. PAUL HOVEY

SATURDAY
Ordinary Time
Week 6

*It is by faith that we understand
that the universe was created
by God's word,
so that what can be seen
was made out of what cannot be seen.*

HEBREWS 11:3

When Columbus
informed the European world
about his discovery of America,
some mapmakers refused
to put the new continent on their maps.
When journalist Ruth Cranston
showed rural Chinese peasants
a photograph of the New York skyline,
they refused to believe it was real.
When the astronauts landed on the moon,
a surprising number of people
believed the whole event was staged
on the back lot of Warner Brothers.

What is one thing that threatens
to keep me from believing
in God and God's word as I should?

*Epochs of faith
are epochs of fruitfulness;
but epochs of unbelief,
however glittering,
are barren of all permanent good.*

JOHANN WOLFGANG VON GOETHE

SUNDAY
Ordinary Time
Week 7 _____

[Jesus said,] "Love your enemies . . . .
and pray for those who mistreat you."
LUKE 6:27-28

In *How to Forgive Your Ex-Husband,*
Marcia Hootman and Patt Perkins
detail the research being done
on the anger of divorced women.
Then they draw two conclusions from it.
First, phenomenal energy and money
are wasted by women trying to get even
with their ex-husbands.
Second, these women are hurt far more
by their anger
than they were by their ex-spouses.
The authors point out that forgiveness
doesn't mean forgoing justice.
They cite Pope John Paul II as an example.
He went to the prison to forgive
his assailant, Mehmet Ali Agca.
"But you notice," they say,
"the pope did not ask
that Agca be let out on parole."

Can I recall a time when I did something
loving toward an enemy or
prayed for someone who mistreated me?

Kindness
is loving people more than they deserve.
JOSEPH JOUBERT

All wisdom comes from the LORD,
and Wisdom is with him forever.

SIRACH 1:1

In his book *Man Does Not Stand Alone,*
A. C. Morrison suggests this experiment.
Mark ten pennies #1 to #10.
Put them in your pocket and shake them.
Now try to draw them out in sequence
from #1 to #10, putting each coin back
after each draw.
The chances of drawing #1 are one in ten.
The chances of drawing #1 and #2
in succession are one in a hundred.
The chances of drawing #1, #2, and #3
in succession are one in a thousand.
The odds continue to mount
until the chances
of drawing #1 to #10 in succession
skyrocket to one in one billion.

How does this experiment suggest that
only the existence of an eternal Wisdom
adequately explains
the existence of our universe?

He has decided the number of the stars
and calls each one by name.
Great and mighty is our Lord;
his wisdom cannot be measured.

PSALM 147:4-5

TUESDAY
Ordinary Time
Week 7

All you that fear the Lord,
trust him,
and you will certainly be rewarded.

SIRACH 2:8

An advertisement for a Greek airline
recalls that after defeating the Trojans,
it took Ulysses ten years
to return home to Greece.
This is because his journey took him
across beautiful blue seas
dotted with 2,000 sun-splashed islands,
30,000 white-sand beaches,
and a never-ending summer.
The advertisement ends by telling us
that all this beauty is the reward
of those who choose to fly to Greece.
The Bible tells us
that an infinitely greater beauty
will be the reward
of those who choose to trust in God.

If someone asked me
why I have chosen to trust God,
what would I say?

I know not where His islands lift
Their fronded palms in air;
I only know I cannot drift
Beyond His love and care.

JOHN GREENLEAF WHITTIER

_Wisdom's servants are the servants
of the Holy One. . . . Those who obey her
will give sound judgments._

SIRACH 4:14-15

An old wise man in ancient China
had one son and one horse.
One day the horse escaped its corral
and fled into the hills.
"Bad luck," said the neighbors.
"How can you be so sure?"
said the old wise man.
Next day the horse returned home,
leading ten wild horses.
"Good luck," said the neighbors.
"How can you be so sure?" said the man.
Next day the man's son was thrown
by a wild horse and broke his leg.
"Bad luck," said the neighbors.
"How can you be so sure?" said the man.
Next day an enemy invaded the village
and led off all able-bodied young men.
The man's injured son was left behind.
This time the neighbors said nothing.

Can I recall something in my life that
began as a cross but ended as a blessing?

_Whoever falls from God's right hand
is caught up in his left._

EDWIN MARKHAM

THURSDAY
Ordinary Time
Week 7 _____

*Delay not your conversion to the LORD,
put it not off from day to day.*

SIRACH 5:8 (NAB)

A day doesn't seem like much time
until you realize
how much can happen in a day.
In his book *In One Day,* Tom Parker says
each day in the United States:
11,000 people get bitten by a dog,
13,000 people get married,
20,000 people write the president,
87,000 people wreck their car,
180,000 people move to a new home.
One day may not seem like much,
but the facts show otherwise.
This is also the point of today's reading:
"Delay not your conversion."
Too much is at stake!

When it comes to my spiritual life,
why do I tend to procrastinate?
What am I delaying right now? Why?

*You wake up in the morning, and lo!
Your purse is magically filled
with twenty-four hours
of the manufactured tissue of your life!
It is yours.
It is the most precious of possessions.*

ARNOLD BENNET

FRIDAY
Ordinary Time
Week 7

A loyal friend is like a safe shelter;
find one, and you have found a treasure.

SIRACH 6:14

Psychologist Eugene Kennedy
has what he calls a "test of friendship."
If you find you can't be with someone
unless you're doing something together,
then that person may not be
as good a friend as you think.
The true test of friendship
is that you can do nothing together
and still be happy.
You enjoy each other so much
that you don't need to add anything
to the glue
that holds your relationship together.

Of all the people I have known,
what one of them
would I like to spend a few hours with
right now? Why?

We are all travellers
in what John Bunyan calls
the wilderness of the world,
and the best we can find in our travels
is an honest friend. He is a fortunate
voyager who finds many.
They keep us worthy of ourselves.

ROBERT LOUIS STEVENSON

SATURDAY
Ordinary Time
Week 7 _____

The LORD formed human beings. . . .
He made them to be like himself.

SIRACH 17:1, 3

Donald Cross Peattie has written
a lot about nature in *Reader's Digest.*
In one article he made this suggestion:
If you ever find a spider spinning a web,
run and get your little boy or girl.
"Lift your child to see.
Tell him that the shining silver
drawn out of the spider's body
has a greater tensile strength than steel.
If he learns admiration
instead of disgust for the tiny spinner,
he will have learned
one of the greatest lessons in nature—
that all life is sacred."
Today, more than ever,
we need to stress that all life—
especially human life—
is a gift from God and is sacred.

To what extent—and why—do I agree
that today, more than ever, we need
to stress the sacredness of life?

By having reverence for life,
we enter into a spiritual relationship
with the world.

ALBERT SCHWEITZER

SUNDAY
Ordinary Time
Week 8

[Jesus said,]
"One blind man cannot lead another one;
if he does, both will fall into a ditch."

LUKE 6:39

Two men on a park bench were arguing
about religion.
The younger one said to the older one,
"You claim you know all about religion.
I'll bet that you don't even know
the Lord's Prayer."
The older man opened his wallet,
put down ten dollars, and snapped,
"This says I do."
The younger man matched him, saying,
"And this says you don't."
The older man began,
"Now I lay me down to sleep . . ."
The younger man handed him
the ten dollars, saying, "You fooled me;
I didn't think you knew it."

How honest am I with other people?
Do I sometimes try to give them
the impression that I know more
about something than I really do know?

We gain more
by letting our real selves be seen,
than by pretending to be what we are not.
FRANCOIS DE LA ROCHEFOUCAULD

MONDAY
Ordinary Time
Week 8 _____

[The Lord] always gives encouragement
to those who are losing hope. . . .
Leave your sin behind.
Pray sincerely that he will help you
live a better life.

SIRACH 17:24-25

A famous painting
portrays an anxious young man
playing chess with the devil for his soul.
The devil has just checkmated
the young man's king.
The average chess player
who studies the painting
sees no hope for the young man.
Paul Murphy, an expert chess player,
studied the painting for a long time.
Suddenly
he saw a way out of the situation.
Excitedly he cried out,
"Don't give up hope, young man.
You still have a good move left!"

What is my greatest source of hope
when I feel checkmated by the devil?

Behind the cloud the starlight lurks,
Through showers the sunbeams fall;
For God, who loveth all His works,
Has left His hope for all.

JOHN GREENLEAF WHITTIER

TUESDAY
Ordinary Time
Week 8

*Give to the Most High
as he has given to you,
just as generously as you can.
The Lord always repays
and will do it many times over.*

SIRACH 35:10-11

Charles Colson
was convicted and sent to prison
for his role
in the Nixon-Watergate scandal.
In his book *Loving God,* Colson described
a woman in a Georgia nursing home.
Athough she was elderly,
and found writing very difficult,
she corresponded with 14 prisoners.
"All of them," she said, "are young and
need a grandmother's love and wisdom.
The difficulty of writing
is such a small 'sacrifice' to make,
if I can help them."

What role
does sacrifice play in my life?

*We ought not to talk of "sacrifice"
when we remember the great sacrifice
which Jesus made by leaving
his Father's throne on high
to give himself for us.*

DAVID LIVINGSTONE

WEDNESDAY
Ordinary Time
Week 8

O Lord God of the universe,
look upon us and have mercy.

SIRACH 36:1

Doing volunteer work
at a home for runaways, Anne Donohue
became angry with God. She wondered,
"Why doesn't God show them the concern
their parents didn't show them?
Why doesn't God show them the love
their parents didn't show them? Why?"
Then it dawned on her!
God wants to do this for them.
But God can do it only through us.
We are God's voice;
we are God's hands; we are God's heart.

When was the last time that someone
heard God speaking through *my* voice,
felt God lifting a burden with *my* hands,
experienced God loving with *my* heart?

Man is on his way to Venus, but he still
hasn't learned to live with his wife.
Man has succeeded in increasing his life
span, yet he exterminates his brothers
six million at a whack.
Man now has the power to destroy
himself and his planet; depend upon it,
he will—should he cease to love.

HARPER LEE

THURSDAY
Ordinary Time
Week 8

*The light of the sun shines down
on everything, and everything is filled
with the Lord's glory.*

SIRACH 42:16

At the age of 44, Carlo Carretto
became a monk
and lived a life of prayer
in the Arabian desert.
In his book *Letters from the Desert,*
he tells how he rediscovered God's glory
in the starry night skies of Arabia:
"How dear they were to me,
those stars. . . . I had come to know them
by their names, then to study them. . . .
Now I could distinguish their color,
their size, their position, their beauty.
I knew my way around them,
and from them I could calculate the time
without a watch."

To what extent do I experience nature
as God's finger motioning to me,
or God's voice speaking to me?

*I love to think of nature
as an unlimited broadcasting system
through which
God speaks to us every hour,
if we only tune in.*

GEORGE WASHINGTON CARVER

FRIDAY
Ordinary Time
Week 8 _____

So let us now give praise to . . .
our ancestors of generations past.

SIRACH 44:1

Africans have a deep appreciation
of the debt they owe their ancestors.
Some tribes
practice a form of ancestor *worship*.
At first this caused a problem
for African converts,
because Christianity teaches
that only God may be *worshiped*.
Now, however,
Christian missionaries build on
the mentality behind this practice
to explain to African converts
the reasons for honoring the saints
and praying for the dead.

How appreciative am I of the debt
I owe people who went before me?
Who is one of these people, and what
debt, especially, do I owe that person?
What is one way I can repay that debt?

No man has come to true greatness
who has not felt in some degree
that his life belongs to his race,
and that what God gives him,
he gives him for mankind.

PHILLIPS BROOKS

SATURDAY
Ordinary Time
Week 8

*I received Wisdom
as soon as I began listening for her,
and I have been rewarded
with great knowledge.*

SIRACH 51:16

People usually associate wisdom
with people who are gray-headed
and have had a lot of experience.
True, there is a wisdom
that comes with age and experience.
But there's also a wisdom
that comes as a gift from God.
Carl Sandburg
refers to this latter wisdom
in one of his writings.
It's about a little girl
watching a military parade.
People are cheering, but she is thinking
about the killing that war involves.
Suddenly she thinks, "I know something.
Someday they're going to hold a war
and nobody will come."

How can I open my heart more fully
to the wisdom that comes
only from God?

*Wisdom has its roots in goodness,
and not goodness its roots in wisdom.*

RALPH WALDO EMERSON

SUNDAY
Ordinary Time
Week 9

[A Roman officer said to Jesus,]
"Just give the order,
and my servant will get well."....
[Jesus said,] "I have never found
faith like this, not even in Israel!"

LUKE 7:7, 9

Frenchman Alexis de Tocqueville wrote
decades ago: "I sought for the genius
and greatness of America . . .
in her fertile fields and
boundless forests—
and it was not there . . .
in her rich mines and her vast world
commerce—and it was not there . . .
in her democratic Congress and
her matchless Constitution—
and it was not there.
Not until I went into the churches
of America . . . did I understand
the secret of her genius and power."

The secret of America's greatness
is etched on her coins: "In God we trust."
How can I deepen my faith and trust
in God—America's faith and trust?

America is great because she is good,
and if America ever ceases to be good,
America will cease to be great.

ALEXIS DE TOCQUEVILLE

MONDAY
Ordinary Time
Week 9

*[The Book of Tobit is a short story
about a Jewish family that was deported
to Assyria by conquering armies.
Tobit remained faithful to his Jewish faith
to the point that he said,]*
"My neighbors [thought] I was crazy."

TOBIT 2:8

After King Solomon died in 922 B.C.,
a civil war split the 12 tribes of Israel
into rival nations: North and South.
In 722 B.C. Assyrian armies conquered
the North and deported the citizens
to Assyria as laborers.
Many of the deported Jews in Assyria
compromised their faith.
Tobit and his wife, Anna, and son, Tobias,
however, remained faithful—
even to the point of suffering ridicule
from their own Jewish neighbors.

How much do I let others influence me
in the practice of my faith?
What is one way
that I tend to compromise my faith?

*Jesus said, "If anyone declares publicly
that he belongs to me,
I will do the same for him
before my Father in heaven."*

MATTHEW 10:32

TUESDAY
Ordinary Time
Week 9 _____

*[Tobit went blind, and his wife
had to work extra hard to support him.
One day a rich person gave her a goat.
Tobit feared that, in her efforts to make
ends meet, she had stolen the goat.
When he voiced his suspicion,
his wife was hurt and deeply angered.]*
*"Now I see what you are really like!"
she shouted. . . . "What about
all those good deeds you used to do?"*
TOBIT 2:14

Sometimes, personal trials
play cruel tricks on us.
In our anguished state of mind,
we let our imaginations and fears
run wild.
We think, do, and say things
that we'd never think, do, or say
under ordinary circumstances.
This happened to Tobit.
Understandably, his wife struck back.

How do I handle
angry remarks or false accusations,
especially when made by loved ones?

*There are two times
when to keep your mouth shut:
when swimming and when angry.*
AUTHOR UNKNOWN

*[After wrongly suspecting
and accusing his wife, Tobit said,]
I was so embarrassed and ashamed
that I sighed and began to cry.
Then . . . I prayed.
[God heard Tobit's prayer and healed him.]*
TOBIT 3:1

In *Who Needs God*,
Rabbi Harold Kushner says
that religion begins with a recognition
of God's greatness and our limitations.
It begins when our ability, confidence,
and security are totally breached.
It begins when we recognize that
"the things that matter most in our lives
are beyond our control.
At the limits of our own power,
we need to turn to a Power
greater than ourselves."

When were my ability, confidence, and
security breached to the point
that I felt the need to turn to a Power
greater than myself? With what results?

*There are no atheists in foxholes
because times like those
bring us face to face
with our limitations.*
RABBI HAROLD KUSHNER

THURSDAY
Ordinary Time
Week 9 _____

[Tobit's son, Tobias, married Sarah.
On their wedding night,
Tobias prayed to God,]
"You said,
'It is not good for man to live alone. . . .'
I have chosen Sarah. . . .
Please be merciful to us and grant
that we may grow old together."

TOBIT 8:6-7

A young man married a great girl.
A family friend said to him,
"You're lucky to have found Maria."
The young man replied, "Lucky?
I've been praying for a great girl
like Maria ever since high school."
The stories of the young man and Maria
and of Tobias and Sarah
should be shared with every teenager.
It could introduce them
to a whole new attitude toward prayer.

How does my own attitude toward prayer
influence my own family interactions?

An anonymous wife
prayed for her husband:
"Lord, place your hand on his shoulder.
Whisper your voice in his ear.
Put your love in his heart.
Help him fulfill your plan in this life."

FRIDAY
Ordinary Time
Week 9

*[Tobit's sight returned
when his son medicated his eyes
according to the instruction of an angel.
Tobit thanked God, saying,]*
*"Praise God.
Praise him for his greatness."*

TOBIT 11:14

Byron Dell grew up on a Nebraska farm.
When he was eight years old,
he had a pony named Frisky,
who sometimes lived up to its name.
One morning Byron was getting the cows
when Frisky became frightened.
Frisky bolted off at breakneck speed.
Byron held on for dear life
and finally got Frisky to stop.
That night before going to bed,
Byron's father knelt down with him
and thanked God that Byron was not hurt.
This incident took place 55 years ago,
but Byron has never forgotten it.
It inspired him to make prayer
a regular part of his daily life.

How comfortable would I be kneeling
and praying with my child or parent?

*My father didn't tell me how to live;
he lived, and let me watch him do it.*
CLARENCE BUDINGTON KELLAND

SATURDAY
Ordinary Time
Week 9 _____

[An angel told Tobit and Tobias,]
"It's a good idea to keep a king's secret,
but what God does
should be told everywhere,
so that he may be praised and honored."

TOBIT 12:7

Missionary doctor Albert Schweitzer
once said in an interview:
"I realize how important to me
were the help, understanding and courage,
the gentleness and wisdom
so many people gave me.
These men and women entered into my life
and became powers within me.
But they never knew it.
Nor did I perceive the real significance
of their help at the time."
What Schweitzer said of those
who touched him deeply, we can say of God.
God entered our life and became
a great reservoir of power within us.
We owe all we have to God and God's grace.

How can I praise and honor God
for all that God has done for me?

"Your light must shine before people,
so that they will see the good things you do
and praise your Father in heaven."

MATTHEW 5:16

SUNDAY
Ordinary Time
Week 10

[Jesus came upon a funeral procession.
The dead man was a widow's only son.
Moved to pity, Jesus said to the boy,]
"Young man! Get up, I tell you!"
The dead man sat up . . . ,
and Jesus gave him back to his mother

LUKE 7:14-15

Jesus' miracles
are the skyrockets of history.
They are the unmistakable "signs"
that a new day has dawned on earth.
Jesus opens the eyes of the blind.
Behind this miracle is a deeper meaning.
It is a "sign" for us to open our eyes
to the new day.
Jesus raises the dead.
Behind it is a deeper meaning, also.
It is a "sign" for us to open ourselves
to the new power present in Jesus and
to let him raise us from death to life.

What tends to keep me
from opening my eyes and myself
to the deeper meaning and message
contained in Jesus' miracles?

The real voyage of discovery
consists not in seeking new lands,
but in seeing with new eyes.

MARCEL PROUST

MONDAY
Ordinary Time
Week 10

[God] helps us in our troubles,
so that we are able to help others . . . ,
using the same help that we ourselves
have received from God.

2 CORINTHIANS 1:4

A minister lost both legs
as a result of war injuries.
He felt useless and discarded.
"Slowly something unexpected happened—
he discovered a whole new ministry.
Doctors asked him to talk with patients
facing similar operations.
Grace came to him in the form
of having to encourage others. . . .
And in the process he was healed."

ROBERT M. HERHOLD

The minister's story illustrates
Paul's point in today's Bible reading.
It also invites me to ask myself,
How has God helped me in a way
that now enables me to help others?

The great day comes when a man
begins to get himself off his hands.
He has lived, let us say, in a mind
like a room surrounded by mirrors. . . .
Now, however, some of the mirrors
change to windows.

HENRY EMERSON FOSDICK

It is God himself
who has set us apart, who has placed
his mark of ownership upon us,
and who has given us the Holy Spirit
in our hearts as the guarantee
of all that he has in store for us.

2 CORINTHIANS 1:21-22

Romans placed a "mark of ownership"
on their slaves and property.
Likewise, Roman generals tattooed
recruits with their "mark of ownership."
Paul had this marking system
in mind when he said that God
"placed his mark of ownership upon us"
when we were baptized.

What is one way I experience
the presence and the power
of the Holy Spirit in my heart—
God's mark of ownership of me?

Faith is not merely praying
Upon our knees at night;
Faith is not merely straying
Through darkness into light. . . .
Faith is the brave endeavor,
The splendid enterprise,
The strength to serve, whatever
Conditions may arise.

ANONYMOUS

WEDNESDAY
Ordinary Time
Week 10 _____

[Paul says of his ministry,]
There is nothing in us
that allows us to claim
that we are capable of doing this work.
The capacity we have comes from God.

2 CORINTHIANS 3:5

Some historians say
that the book *Uncle Tom's Cabin*
did more to end slavery in America
than any other single force.
But Harriet Beecher Stowe refused
to take credit for the book, saying,
"The Lord wrote it,
and I was the humblest instrument
of his hand."
Paul says something similar
about his ministry in today's reading.

How much credit do I give to God
for talents? For my achievements?

It is from
out of the depths of our humanity
that the heights of our destiny
look grandest.
Let me truly feel that in myself
I am nothing, and at once,
through every inlet of my soul,
God comes in, and is everything in me.

WILLIAM MOUNTFORD

THURSDAY
Ordinary Time
Week 10

*God in his mercy
has given us this work to do,
and so we do not become discouraged. . . .
For it is not ourselves that we preach;
we preach Jesus Christ.*

2 CORINTHIANS 4.1, 5

"The Christian faith
is firmly rooted in the incarnation,
in the conviction
that 'God was in Christ
reconciling the world unto himself.'
To believe in Christ is to believe
that God has come to earth. . . .
In Christ, we meet the living God.
Jesus is more than a religious genius
or a holy man or a spiritual pioneer.
To believe in Christ is to believe
that the living God has come."
EARLE W. CRAWFORD, *Pulpit Preaching*

What convinces me most
that Jesus is more than a holy man,
a religious genius,
or a spiritual pioneer?

*Do not be afraid   I am with you!
I am your God—let nothing terrify you!
I will make you strong and help you;
I will protect you and save you.*

ISAIAH 41:10

FRIDAY
Ordinary Time
Week 10 ⎯⎯⎯⎯⎯⎯⎯⎯⎯⎯

[Paul writes of his trials,]
We are often troubled, but not crushed . . .
and though badly hurt at times,
we are not destroyed.

2 CORINTHIANS 4:8-9

A letter of Saint Francis de Sales
describes a custom of farmers in his day.
When they carried water in a bucket,
they floated a piece of wood on the water
to keep it from splashing up and out.
That piece of wood is a lot like Jesus;
and the splashing water, a lot like life.
Whenever the waters of life
splash about, threatening to destroy us,
we need only turn to Jesus.
He will calm them as he calmed the sea.
He will give us serenity
in the face of trouble and trials—
just as he did for Paul.

With what kind of trust
do I turn to Jesus in times of trial?

Like an ant on a stick
both ends of which are burning,
I go to and fro without knowing
what to do and in great despair. . . .
Graciously look upon me.
Thy love is my refuge.

ANONYMOUS INDIAN AUTHOR

When anyone is joined to Christ,
he is a new being;
the old is gone, the new has come.
All this is done by God,
who through Christ changed us.

2 CORINTHIANS 5:17-18

John Powell tells about a young man
who for almost 18 years
could see only a few feet in front of him.
When he finally got glasses,
he was amazed
at how beautiful everything was.
He said, "Getting glasses was
the second most beautiful experience
of my life."
"What was the first?" asked John.
The young man replied,
"The day I came to believe in Jesus
and saw that God is truly my Father.
It was like beginning a new life."

Did I ever have a spiritual experience
that impacted me in a memorable way?
When and where did it take place?

Fear not
that your life shall come to an end,
but rather
that it shall never have a beginning.

JOHN HENRY NEWMAN

SUNDAY
Ordinary Time
Week 11 _____

*[A sinful woman fell at the feet of Jesus
and began washing them with her tears.]
Jesus said to the woman,
"Your sins are forgiven."*

LUKE 7:48

In *All Quiet on the Western Front*,
a young German soldier lies in a crater,
taking cover from artillery fire.
Suddenly a French soldier leaps into
the same crater, taking cover also.
The German youth bayonets and kills him.
This is the first man he has killed,
and he wonders what his name is.
Seeing a wallet in the dead man's pocket,
he takes it out. In it is a photograph
of a young mother holding a child.
The German gets a lump in his throat.
The dead man is not an enemy
but a father and husband like himself—
someone who loves and is loved.
This *new vision* of his one-time "enemy"
makes forgiveness and love possible.

What might I do to change my *vision*
of someone I ought to forgive,
as Jesus has forgiven that same person?

*To forgive is to set a prisoner free
and to discover that the prisoner is ME.*

AUTHOR UNKNOWN

We seem poor,
but we make many people rich;
we seem to have nothing,
yet we really possess everything.

2 CORINTHIANS 6:10

A missionary on a Pacific island
was deeply moved when a girl presented
him with a lovely seashell.
"Where did you get such a lovely shell?"
the missionary asked.
The girl explained
that she had walked many miles
to a bay across the island,
to the only place shells are found.
"How wonderful of you to go so far
to get me such a lovely gift,"
said the missionary.
A huge grin lit up the girl's face
as she said,
"Long walk, part of gift."

What is one gift that I might give today
that would cost me little or no money,
but that would make another person
extremely happy? Who? Why?

Rings and jewels are not gifts,
but apologies for gifts.
The only gift is a part of thyself.

RALPH WALDO EMERSON

TUESDAY
Ordinary Time
Week 11 _____

We want you to know
what God's grace has accomplished
in the churches in Macedonia. . . .
They were extremely generous . . .
even though they are very poor. . . .
They gave . . . more than they could.

2 CORINTHIANS 8:1–3

Jack Benny was a popular comedian
in the early days of radio.
One recurring theme in his humor
was his stinginess.
For example, on one show
a thief put a gun to his head and said,
"Your life or your money?"
Benny didn't answer.
Again, the thief repeated his demand,
"Your life or your money?"
Again, Benny didn't answer.
Now the thief became angry, saying,
"Your life or your money!"
Benny answered, "Give me time;
I'm still thinking."

How much of a "Jack Benny spirit"
do I have in me? For example?

Most people think that "holding on"
is the key to happiness.
Actually, the reverse is true.
The key is "letting go."

*Remember that the person
who plants few seeds
will have a small crop;
the one who plants many seeds
will have a large crop.*

2 CORINTHIANS 9:6

A little incident played a big role
in the murder conviction of Judd Gray.
On the night of the crime, near the site
of the murder, Gray got into a taxi.
The question was whether the driver
remembered his face well enough
to make a positive identification.
It turned out that he could.
When the taxi driver dropped Gray off,
Gray gave him a nickle tip.
The amazed cabbie said,
"I wanted to get a good look at his face.
I'll never forget him."
Then, pointing to Gray, he said,
"That's him right there!"

How generous am I with my time, talent,
and treasure?

*I'd rather be a beggar
and spend my last dollar like a king,
than be a king
and spend my money like a beggar.*

ROBERT G. INGERSOLL

THURSDAY
Ordinary Time
Week 11 _____

You accept a spirit and a gospel
completely different from the Spirit
and the gospel you received from us!

2 CORINTHIANS 11:4

Charles Colson
was a top White House aide in the 1970s.
He was convicted and imprisoned
in the Watergate scandal.
Later he had a religious conversion.
Now he crisscrosses the nation
preaching the "grassroots" gospel of Jesus.
He speaks out, especially, against
TV preachers of the far right,
who preach a "prosperity" gospel—
a gospel that "honors excessive wealth
as a sign of God's favor and leaves the
poor to fend for themselves" (JOE WILLIS).
Colson protests their thesis:
If you live a "good life," God will bless
you with material wealth and success.
Colson says, "God doesn't
want successes. He wants us."

How do I interpret Jesus' words:
"How hard it is for those who have wealth
to enter the kingdom of God!" (LUKE 18:24)?

[Jesus said,] "Your heart
will always be where your riches are."

LUKE 12:34

*[Paul writes,] Five times I was given
the thirty-nine lashes by the Jews;
three times I was whipped by the Romans.*
2 CORINTHIANS 11:24-25

Tennis star Alice Marble woke up
to what she hoped would be a glorious day
in her life. She was playing
in England's Wimbledon finals.
Then came the shock of her life.
She felt a stabbing pain in her stomach.
Minutes later
a doctor diagnosed it as a torn muscle.
When Alice insisted on playing,
the doctor told her she was foolish.
She wrote later,
"I shall never forget . . . that first game.
Every swing . . . made me want to scream."
Incredibly, Alice went on to win
while the Queen of England and
20,000 unsuspecting spectators watched.

Marble's readiness to suffer to win and
Paul's readiness to suffer for Christ
invite me to inventory my readiness to
suffer for the spread of God's kingdom.

*Christ himself suffered for you
and left you an example,
so that you would follow in his steps.*
1 PETER 2:21

SATURDAY
Ordinary Time
Week 11 _____

[Paul asked God to remove a painful
ailment from his life; but God said,]
"My grace is all you need, for my power
is greatest when you are weak."

2 CORINTHIANS 12:9

Correspondent Terry Anderson
of the Associated Press was kidnapped
by Shiite Muslim extremists in 1985.
He spent the next seven years
in windowless cells, often in chains.
He nearly despaired in December 1987,
banging his head against the wall
until he bled. Later he said,
"I think we come closest to God
at our lowest moments. It's easiest
to hear God when you are stripped
of pride, arrogance;
when you have nothing to rely on
except God. It's pretty painful
to get to that point, but when you do,
God is there."

Can I recall one of the lowest moments
in life? How did this experience
affect my relationship with God?

In the midst of winter,
I finally learned that there was in me
an invincible summer.

ALBERT CAMUS

SUNDAY
Ordinary Time
Week 12

[Jesus said,]
"Whoever wants to save his own life
will lose it, but whoever loses his life
for my sake will save it."

LUKE 9:24

Vance Havner writes:
"God uses broken things.
It takes broken soil to produce a crop,
broken clouds to give rain,
broken grain to give bread,
broken bread to give strength.
It is a broken alabaster jar
that gives forth perfume. . . .
It is Peter weeping bitterly,
who returns to greater power."
True spiritual strength
lies not in holding on to things
but in letting go of them.
Only by "letting go and letting God"
can we open ourselves
to a greater power than our own.
The paradox of Christianity is, indeed,
we are strongest when we are weakest.

How might the words
"letting go and letting God"
apply to my life at this very moment?

Lord, give me the courage to let go
and give you total control of my life.

MONDAY
Ordinary Time
Week 12

The LORD said to Abram,
"Leave your country,
your relatives, and your father's home,
and go to a land
that I am going to show you."

GENESIS 12:1

Father John Catoir
describes his call to the ministry
in his book *That Your Joy May Be Full*.
He says that as a youth he was attracted
to the priesthood but held back.
He was afraid of the
"alligators in the swamp," as he put it.
Seven years later,
after college and military service,
he had the courage to face the alligators.
He writes:
"I never regretted that decision.
Once I decided to put my hand in God's,
I knew I was safe. I knew I had
something more dependable
than human assurances."

What keeps me from putting my hand
in God's hand, to be guided to whatever
"country" God will show me?

Remember, I will be with you
and protect you wherever you go.

GENESIS 28:15

TUESDAY
Ordinary Time
Week 12

[Abram and Lot traveled together.
But as their cattle and families grew,
there wasn't enough pasture.] So quarrels
broke out. . . . Abram said to Lot . . . ,
"Choose any part of the land you want.
You go one way, and I'll go the other."

GENESIS 13:7-9

The great African leader Paul Kruger
lived at the turn of the century.
One day he was called upon to divide
some land between feuding brothers.
Because the land contained hills, lakes,
and mines, he realized
that almost any division he would make
would be hotly contested.
Kruger pondered the problem deeply.
Then he hit upon a solution.
He called the brothers together,
had one of them divide the land,
and gave the other one first choice
of the half that he wanted.

How do I handle disputes that involve me,
or that arise among those around me?
What improvements might I make?

The place to be happy is here.
The time to be happy is now.
The way to be happy is to make others so.
ROBERT C. INGERSOLL

WEDNESDAY
Ordinary Time
Week 12 _____

[Abram was old and childless.
One night God told him,] "Look at the sky
and try to count the stars; you will have
as many descendants as that."
Abram put his trust in the LORD.

GENESIS 15:5-6

Several thrill seekers
had crossed Niagara Falls on a tightrope.
One of them decided to "up the ante"
and push a person across in a wheelbarrow.
He practiced daily with a load of gravel.
Someone who'd been watching him said,
"You're ready! All you need now
is a man who trusts you enough to sit
in the wheelbarrow."
"Are you absolutely sure I'm ready?"
asked the daredevil. "Yes!" said the man.
"Good!" said the daredevil.
"Get in the wheelbarrow!"

God is not a daredevil,
but God is looking for believers who
trust enough to "get in the wheelbarrow"
and dare great things for the kingdom.
How ready am I?

How calmly ought I to place myself
into the hands of the One
who holds the world in loving hands?

ANONYMOUS

THURSDAY
Ordinary Time
Week 12

*Abram's wife Sarai had not borne him
any children. But she had an Egyptian
slave girl named Hagar, and so she said
to Abram, . . ."Why don't you sleep with
my slave girl? Perhaps she can have a child
for me." . . . Hagar bore Abram a son,
and he named him Ishmael.*

GENESIS 16:1-2, 15

Archaeologists unearthed clay tablets
in modern Iraq that date to Abram.
Among them is a marriage contract.
It states that a sterile wife
is obligated to provide her husband
with a substitute wife for childbearing.
This explains the puzzling episode
in today's Bible reading.
Interestingly, Arabs and Jews
both claim descendancy from Abram:
Arabs, through Ishmael;
Jews, through Isaac,
who was later born to Sarai.

How do I resolve puzzling questions
that arise in my reading of the Bible?
What keeps me from listing them
and asking someone about them?

*Learning is like rowing upstream;
not to advance is to drop back.*

CHINESE PROVERB

FRIDAY
Ordinary Time
Week 12 _____

*[God told Abram (Abraham) that Sarai
(Sarah) would bear a son.] Abraham bowed
down with his face touching the ground,
but he began to laugh when he thought,
"Can a man have a child
when he is a hundred years old?"*

GENESIS 17:17

Today's Bible passage
causes us to do a double take.
When God says that Sarah will
bear him a son, what does Abraham do?
Does he praise God for deciding
to do such a marvelous thing?
Does he thank God for deciding
to bless him so splendidly?
Does he rush to tell Sarah the news?
No! Abraham laughs and says to himself,
"Can a child be born to a man
who is a hundred years old?"
God's reaction to Abraham's incredulity
is just as provocative: God ignores it,
as a loving parent ignores
the foolishness of an immature child.

How patient am I with the foolish antics
of insensitive or immature people?

*Patience is the ability to idle your motor
when you feel like stripping your gears.*

AUTHOR UNKNOWN

[When she heard she was to bear a son,
Sarah reacted as Abraham did.]
Sarah laughed. . . .
Then the LORD asked Abraham, . . .
"Is anything too hard for the LORD?"

GENESIS 18:12-14

In 1842, the U.S. Congress laughed
when Samuel Morse explained his ideas
for sending messages through wire.
In 1878, the British Parliament laughed
when Thomas Edison explained his ideas
for creating light in a glass container.
In 1908, a J. P. Morgan official laughed
when Billy Durant suggested that
half a million cars a year would someday
travel the roads in this country.

When I hear someone—
especially a young person—
express an idea that I don't
fully comprehend or agree with,
how do I usually react?
How should I react? Why?

A new idea is delicate.
It can be killed by a sneer or a yawn;
it can be stabbed to death by a quip
and worried to death by a frown
on the right person's brow.

CHARLES BROWER

SUNDAY
Ordinary Time
Week 13 _____

[Jesus said,]
"Anyone who . . . keeps looking back
is of no use for the Kingdom of God."

LUKE 9:62

Bela Karolyi was a gymnastics coach
for Rumania in the days
of Communism and the Iron Curtain.
He developed such Olympic stars
as gold-medalist Nadia Comenici.
His international fame
won him special government favors,
including such things as a Mercedes—
unheard of in Communist countries.
Then in 1981 he decided
to turn his back on Communism
and seek a free life in the West.
When the "zero hour" for leaving came,
Bela did not look back
at his state favors, his Mercedes,
and his celebrity status.
He simply walked straight ahead,
carrying only a small suitcase.

Bela Karolyi is a perfect image of the
kind of follower Jesus had in mind.
How closely do I mirror that image?

Strong lives
are motivated by dynamic purposes.
KENNETH HILDEBRAND

[God promised Abraham,]
"I will not destroy [Sodom]
if there are ten [good people in it."
But ten good people could not be found.]

GENESIS 18:32

Benjamin Franklin was a talented printer,
inventor, and writer.
He penned this provocative passage
in *Poor Richard's Almanack:*
"For want of a nail a shoe was lost.
For want of a shoe a horse was lost.
For want of a horse a rider was lost.
For want of a rider a battle was lost.
For want of a battle a kingdom was lost—
And all for want of a horseshoe nail."

The loss of a kingdom for want of a nail
and God's inability to find ten good people
invite me to ask, What motivates me
to do what I think is right,
even when I am alone or in the minority?

Cowardice asks . . . "Is it safe?"
Expedience asks . . . . "Is it politic?"
Vanity asks . . . "Is it popular?" . . .
There comes a time
when one must take a position
that is neither safe, politic, nor popular,
but one must take it because it is right.

MARTIN LUTHER KING, JR.

TUESDAY
Ordinary Time
Week 13 —————————————————

Suddenly the LORD rained burning sulfur
on the cities of Sodom and Gommorah
and destroyed them. . . .
[Abraham] saw smoke rising from the land,
like smoke from a huge furnace.

GENESIS 19:24-25, 28

Some Bible readers think an earthquake
(common to the area)
touched off the fiery holocaust.
Words like "burning sulfur" and "smoke"
suggest that coal and petroleum deposits
(still found in the area)
exploded during the earthquake,
igniting the inferno described.
Regardless of what happened,
the point is clear: Sodom and Gommorah
met with a terrible destruction,
which the biblical author interpreted
as God's judgment upon them.

What message might I take away from
the story of Sodom and Gommorah?

More and more of the decisions
which effect human lives
will be scientific decisions.
They must not be made by persons
who are not equipped to understand
the moral consequences.

DR. AARON IHDE

[When Sarah seemed sterile,
Abraham had Ishmael by Hagar.
Later, Sarah bore Isaac and]
Abraham gave a great feast.

GENESIS 21:8

Paul used this analogy
in preaching to the Jews of his time:
Hagar represents the Old Covenant
mediated by Moses on Mount Sinai.
Hagar's son, Ishmael, represents Jews,
who were made God's children
by the Moses-mediated covenant.
Sarah, on the other hand, represents
the New Covenant mediated by Jesus
at the Last Supper in Jerusalem.
Sarah's son, Isaac, represents Christians,
who were made God's children
by the Jesus-mediated covenant.
Paul's point? As Isaac became the new
inheritor of God's promise to Abraham,
so did the children of the New Covenant.
GALATIANS 4:21-27

What is one way I can better
express my gratitude for being made
a child of God by the covenant
mediated at the Last Supper?

Gratitude is the memory of the heart.
JEAN BAPTISTE MASSIEU

THURSDAY
Ordinary Time
Week 13 _____

God tested Abraham [saying] . . .
"Go to the land of Moriah. . . .
On a mountain that I will show you,
offer [Isaac] as a sacrifice to me."
[Abraham obeyed, taking Isaac with him.]
GENESIS 22:1-2

Faith in God
involves trust and risk on our part.
First, it involves *trust.*
For example, *reason* told Abraham
that if he sacrificed Isaac,
God's promise of numerous descendants
through Isaac could not be fulfilled.
Abraham's *faith,* however, enabled him
to trust God rather than his own reason.
Second, faith involves *risk.*
For example, when two people marry,
neither is certain that the other
will remain faithful in a major crisis.
But faith in each other enables them
to take this risk freely and gladly.
Faith in God is something like that.

When I imagine myself to be Abraham,
what are my thoughts
as God tells me to sacrifice Isaac?
What motivates me to obey?

Little love; little trust.
ENGLISH PROVERB

[Isaac was deeply saddened
by the death of his mother, Sarah.
Then one day he met Rebecca.]
Isaac loved Rebecca, and so he was
comforted for the loss of his mother.

GENESIS 24:67

There was a time when it seemed
that singer Willie Nelson's career
was almost totally wrecked.
Then came a turnaround.
Willie talked about it in an interview
with Barbara Walters.
He said the power to reverse everything
came from the love of his wife.
At that point in the interview,
he sang Barbara the song he wrote
to celebrate his wife's love for him.
It is called
"Angel Flying Too Close to the Ground,"
and contains this beautiful line:
"Love is the greatest healer to be found."
It was this kind of healing power
that Rebecca's love brought to Isaac
after his mother's death.

How have I been healed by another's love?
How have I healed another by my love?

Love is God's shadow in our universe.

ANONYMOUS

258

[Isaac had two sons:
Esau, the firstborn, and Jacob.
When Isaac was old and blind,
it became time to give the blessing
that would transfer his authority
to his firstborn.
Jacob tricked his blind father
into believing that he was Esau.]
So [Isaac] gave him his blessing.

GENESIS 27:27

This story gives us an insight
into how God dealt with biblical peoples.
God didn't manipulate them like puppets.
God didn't program them,
as we program a computer.
On the contrary, God gave them
the same freedom that we have.
In other words, God worked through their
free actions, even when these were sinful.
This story contains an important lesson:
Nothing—not even sin—
can frustrate God's plan of salvation.

How truly do I believe that God wants
to use me to achieve great things—
in spite of my sinfulness?

Today's opportunities
erase yesterday's failures.
GENE BROWN

[Jesus sent his disciples to preach
the Good News to all, telling them,]
"Whenever you go into a house,
first say, 'Peace be with this house.' "
LUKE 10:5

Helen Keller could neither see nor hear.
Yet she became a great public speaker.
One night after a lecture
someone asked her this question:
"If you could have one wish granted,
what would it be?"
The questioner thought Helen might say,
"I'd wish for the ability to see and hear."
But she said, "I'd wish for world peace."
Jesus would have applauded
Helen Keller's beautiful response.
For that is what he told his followers
to be: instruments of peace.
"Happy are those who work for peace,"
Jesus told the crowds on the mountain.
"God will call them his children!"
(MATTHEW 5:9).

How much of an instrument of God's
peace am I in my workplace? My home?
How might I become a better one?

You can't shake hands
with a clenched fist.
INDIRA GANDHI

MONDAY
Ordinary Time
Week 14 _____

[One night Jacob camped under the stars.
In a dream, he saw God.
That dream changed his entire life.]
Jacob woke up and said,
"The LORD is here!
[The LORD] is in this place!"

GENESIS 28:16

A high school student
wrote in a homework assignment:
"I was skiing all alone down a slope.
Suddenly, I pulled up and stopped.
I still don't know why;
it was like someone said, 'Stop, Chris!'
Everything was quiet and beautiful:
the clear blue sky above me,
the soft white snow below me,
and green cedars on each side of me.
As I stood there,
a strange feeling came over me,
and a strange thought entered my mind:
'God is here with me!'
It was a moment I'll never forget."

What is the closest I ever came
to an experience such as that described
by the student and by Jacob?

I have always regarded nature
as the clothing of God.
ALAN HOVHANESS

TUESDAY
Ordinary Time
Week 14

[A mysterious being told Jacob,]
"Your name will no longer be Jacob. . . .
Your name will be Israel."

GENESIS 32:28

In biblical times,
names did more than identify people.
Names often revealed something of them.
Concerning Mary's child, Joseph was told
in a dream, "You will name him Jesus—
because he will save people
from their sins" (MATTHEW 1:21).
Similarly, in biblical times a name change
indicated a change in a person.
When Abram and Sarai
were chosen to parent a great nation,
God renamed them Abraham and Sarah.
This background helps us understand
Jacob's name change to *Israel*.
He is now the official bearer
of God's promise to his father, Abraham.
He is to father twelve sons, who will
father the twelve tribes of Israel,
who will be known as *Israelites*.

At baptism I was renamed *Christian*.
What does this name reveal about me?
How well am I living up to my calling?

The believers were . . . called Christians.

ACTS 11:26

WEDNESDAY
Ordinary Time
Week 14 ——————

*[Israel's favorite son was Joseph.
His angry brothers sold him into slavery,
saying wild animals devoured him.
Joseph went to Egypt, where events put
him in charge of food during a famine.
When Joseph's brothers came for food,
Joseph recognized them (but they didn't
recognize him). To test them,
Joseph jailed them on false charges.
Overhearing their conversation in jail,
Joseph learned that they were truly sorry
for causing their father such pain
by saying that Joseph had been killed.
Moved by their sorrow, he] began to cry.*

GENESIS 42:24

In the film *The Karate Kid,*
Mr. Miyagi asks Daniel for his reason
for wanting to learn karate.
Daniel says, "Is revenge sufficient reason?"
Mr. Miyagi replies, "Who seeks revenge
should dig two graves: one for his enemy
and one for himself."

Joseph's example and Mr. Miyagi's advice
to Daniel invite me to inventory
my response to those who injure me.

*Do not let evil defeat you;
instead, conquer evil with good.*

ROMANS 12:21

[Joseph revealed himself,
wept with his brothers, and told them,]
"Do not be upset or blame yourselves
because you sold me here.
It was really God who sent me
ahead of you to save people's lives."

GENESIS 45:5

British journalist Douglas Hyde
sought to smear the Catholic Church,
so he got the book *The Catholic Church*
Against the Twentieth Century
by Avro Manhattan.
As he read it, something unexpected
happened to him. He writes:
"Instead of giving me ammunition . . .
I learned, despite the tendentious writing,
something of the Church's social teachings.
It was written to make anti-Catholics.
It helped make me 'pro' instead."
Something like that
happened to Joseph's brothers.
They set out to frame their brother
but ended up falling in love with him.

When bad things happen to me,
how open am I to the possibility
that God can bring good out of them?

There's no sorrow heaven can't heal.

THOMAS MORE (slightly adapted)

FRIDAY
Ordinary Time
Week 14 _____

Joseph got in his chariot
and went to Goshen to meet his father.
When they met, Joseph threw his arms
around his father's neck
and cried for a long time.

GENESIS 46:29

This beautiful expression of affection
stands out in stark contrast to the way
many modern family members
(especially fathers and sons)
express their affection for one another.
For example, not long ago a father wrote
to Ann Landers about his dead son:
"The greatest regret of my life
is that I kept my son at arm's length.
I believed it was unmanly for males
to show affection for one another.
I treated my son
the way my father treated me,
and I realize now
what a terrible mistake it was."

Toward what family member
do I find it easiest
to express my affection? Why?

Our children give us an opportunity
to become the parents
we always wish we had.

NANCY SEMALIN

*[When Israel (Jacob) died,
Joseph's brothers were afraid that Joseph
might turn on them.
Hearing of their fear, Joseph said to them,]*
*"You have nothing to fear.
I will take care of you and your children."*

GENESIS 50:21

Corrie ten Boom survived imprisonment
by the Nazis in World War II.
After the war she toured Europe,
lecturing on forgiveness of enemies.
One night in Munich she met a hated
guard from the prison she had been in.
When she couldn't take his hand
in a gesture of forgiveness, she prayed.
At that moment some mysterious power
helped her reach out forgivingly to him.
That episode taught Corrie a great truth:
The same Jesus who tells us to forgive
will give us the grace to do it.
We need only open our hearts to it.

Who are two people who have hurt me?
What keeps me from telling Jesus
that I forgive them and asking him
to bless them in a special way?

*Forgive one another
just as the Lord has forgiven you.*
COLOSSIANS 3:13

SUNDAY
Ordinary Time
Week 15 ——————————————

*[Praising the Good Samaritan's kindness,
Jesus said,]* "Go . . . and do the same."

LUKE 10:37

Glamour magazine for December 1991
carried an editorial
about a lady in a red car.
She drove up to the Bay Bridge tollbooth,
gave the attendant seven tickets, and said,
"I'm paying for the next six cars."
As each car stopped, the driver was told,
"The lady in the red car paid your toll.
Have a nice day!"
The lady in the red car was inspired
by a sentence penned by Anne Herbert:
"Practice random kindness
and senseless acts of beauty."
Anne believes that "random kindness"
is capable of generating a tidal wave,
just as "random violence" is.
Maybe that's why Anne's lovely sentence
is starting to show up in a lot of places.
It awakens something
deep inside the human heart.

How might I "go . . . and do the same"?

*Like all revolutions,
guerilla goodness begins slowly,
with a single act. Let it be yours.*

GLAMOUR magazine

[Joseph's popularity led many Israelites
to migrate to and settle in Egypt.
They prospered.] Then, a new king,
who knew nothing about Joseph,
came to power in Egypt. He said . . . ,
"These Israelites are . . . a threat. . . ."
So the Egyptians put slave drivers
over them to crush their spirits
with hard labor. The Israelites built
the cities of Pithom and Rameses.

EXODUS 1:8-9, 11

Archaeology supports this account.
An ancient stone carving of Rameses II
says, "He built the city of Rameses
with Asiatic Semetic slaves."
An ancient Egyptian tomb painting
shows Semetic-looking slaves
making bricks.
Shalom Asch's novel *Moses* portrays
the sad plight of the Israelite slaves:
"Their bodies . . . glistened like copper. . . .
They did their work in dull silence . . .
under the threat of whips."

Who in modern society is being oppressed
in a way not unlike the Israelites? Why?

The function of freedom
is to free somebody else.
TONI MORRISON

TUESDAY
Ordinary Time
Week 15 _____

*[Authorities
tried to kill the infant Moses.
Likewise, they] tried to have
[the adult] Moses killed, but Moses fled.*

EXODUS 2:15

There is a remarkable parallel
between the lives of Moses and Jesus.
Authorities tried to kill the infant Jesus
(MATTHEW 2:13), just as they had tried
to kill the infant Moses (EXODUS 1:22).
So, too, the adult Jesus had to flee
for his life (LUKE 4:29, JOHN 8:59),
just as the adult Moses did.
Similarly, both Jesus and Moses
played similar roles in life.
Both served as lawgivers
(MATTHEW 5, DEUTERONOMY 5),
and both were covenant mediators
(LUKE 22:20, DEUTERONOMY 5).

How dedicated am I to the role in life
that God has given me—
especially when it comes to my family?

*To be a Christian . . . is not simply
to believe with one's mind, but also
to become a doer of the word . . . even if
that leads to the path of persecution
and the possibility of martyrdom.*

U.S. BISHOPS, *The Challenge of Peace*

WEDNESDAY
Ordinary Time
Week 15

Moses saw that the bush was on fire
but that it was not burning up.
"This is strange," he thought....
"I will go closer and see."...
God said, "Do not come any closer....
You are standing on holy ground.
I am the God ...
of Abraham, Isaac, and Jacob."
So Moses covered his face.

EXODUS 3:2-3, 5-6

In the Bible, fire is a common signal
of God's presence.
A column of fire guides Israel
through the desert (EXODUS 13:21).
A fiery smoke indicates God's presence
on Mount Sinai when Moses receives
the Ten Commandments (EXODUS 19:18).
The Holy Spirit comes upon the disciples
in tongues of fire (ACTS 2:3).

What is unique about fire that makes it
a fitting indicator of God's presence?

Earth's crammed with heaven,
And every common bush afire with God;
But only he who sees
*   takes off his shoes;*
The rest sit round it
*   and pluck blackberries.*

E. B. BROWNING

THURSDAY
Ordinary Time
Week 15

God said, "I am who I am. . . .
'The one who is called I AM
has sent me to you.'
Tell the Israelites that I, the LORD . . .
have sent you to them.
This is my name forever."

EXODUS 3:14-15

The expression "I am who I am"
introduces the Hebrew name for God.
Designated by the four letters *YHWH,*
it is usually translated "Lord" in English.
God's unusual name suggests
that "God is who God is and that's it."
God can neither be named nor defined.
Anything said about God
falls infinitely short of the reality.
Saint Augustine put it well, saying,
"We know God more
by what God is not than by what God is."
The expression "God is infinite" simply
means God is *not finite* as humans are.
The expression "God is all-knowing"
simply means God is not limited
in knowledge as humans are.

How do I image God when I pray?

God has suffered from too many attempts
to define the undefinable.

JERRY HANSPICKER

FRIDAY
Ordinary Time
Week 15

[The LORD said, "Slay a lamb,]
take some of the blood and put it
on the doorposts . . . of the houses
in which the animals are to be eaten. . . .
When I see the blood,
I will pass over you and will not harm you
when I punish the Egyptians. . . .
Celebrate this day [the Passover]
as a religious festival . . . for all time."

EXODUS 12:7, 13–14

Saint Paul called Jesus
"our Passover lamb" (1 CORINTHIANS 5:7).
As the blood of the first "Passover lamb"
saved Israel
from physical slavery and death,
so the blood of "our Passover lamb"
saves us from spiritual slavery and death.
And as the first Passover lamb's flesh
was eaten by the first Israelites,
so the flesh of "our Passover lamb"
is eaten by us (JOHN 6:54–56).

Jesus, help me appreciate how well
the two testaments fit together.

In the Old Testament,
the New Testament lies concealed;
in the New Testament,
the Old Testament lies revealed.

SAINT AUGUSTINE

SATURDAY
Ordinary Time
Week 15 _____

*[When the time to flee from Egypt came,
the Israelites left] so suddenly that they
did not have time to get their food ready.*
                                    EXODUS 12:37, 39

Imagine you must flee for your life.
Your only escape is into vast desert.
As you head into the hostile wasteland,
you realize that your life
is now endangered in a new way.
You have no idea what lies before you
or where food and drink are to be found.
The Israelites faced a situation like this
when they fled Egypt and disappeared
into the wasteland of the Sinai desert.
They were repeating the "faith journey"
God asked their father Abraham to make
years before them.
It is the same faith journey
God asks each one of us to make.

What do I find most difficult in my
faith journey? Why this?

*Without somehow destroying me
in the process,
how could God reveal himself in a way
that would leave no room for doubt?
If there would be no room for doubt,
there would be no room for me.*

                                    FREDERICK BUECHNER

*[Martha complained to Jesus because
Mary visited with him while she worked.
Jesus replied,] "Martha, Martha! . . .
Mary has chosen the right thing,
and it will not be taken away from her."*

LUKE 10:41-42

A young monk had questions
about his order's motto: "Pray and Work."
So one day the abbot invited him
to row across the lake with him.
The abbot rowed first—but with one oar.
As a result the boat went in circles,
and they made no progress.
The young monk said,
"Abbot, unless you row with both oars,
you won't get anywhere."
The abbot replied, "You're so right, son!
The right oar is prayer; the left is work.
Unless you use them together,
you just go in circles."

What balance do I try to keep
between work and prayer? How do I
know when the balance is correct?

*Each Christian
needs half an hour of prayer each day,
except when we are busy;
then we need an hour.*

SAINT FRANCIS DE SALES

MONDAY
Ordinary Time
Week 16 _____

[Problems arose after Moses
led the Israelites out of slavery in Egypt
to freedom in the desert. They said,]
"Did you have to bring us out here
in the desert to die? . . .
Didn't we tell you . . . this would happen?"
EXODUS 14:11-12

Time magazine ran a cover story
called "Rocky Mountain High."
It eulogized the beauty and majesty
of this popular vacation area.
Sandwiched into the story
was a remark by Daniel Webster,
our nation's secretary of state in 1852:
"What do we want
with this worthless area,
this region of savages and wild beasts,
of shifting sands and whirlwinds of dust,
of cactus and prairie dogs?
To what use could we ever hope
to put these great deserts
and these endless mountain ranges?"
Moses met similar negative criticism.

How much do I let the negative or critical
attitudes of others impact my actions?

How far would Moses have gone
if he had taken a poll in Egypt?
HARRY TRUMAN

*[A worried crowd of Israelites
arrived at the shore of the Red Sea.
The Egyptians were in hot pursuit.
God told Moses to hold out his staff.
Moses trusted and the Red Sea divided,
making a path for the anxious Israelites
but swallowing up the Egyptians.]
Then Moses and the Israelites
sang this song to the LORD:
"I will sing to the LORD,
because he has won a glorious victory."*

EXODUS 15:1

"Overhead in an Orchard" is a poem
by Elizabeth Cheney. It reads:
"Said the Robin to the Sparrow:
'I should really like to know
Why these anxious human beings
Rush about and worry so.'
Said the Sparrow to the Robin:
'Friend, I think that it must be
That they have no heavenly Father
Such as cares for you and me.' "

How would I answer the Robin?
What is the Sparrow's point?

*Don't tell me that worry doesn't do
any good. I know better.
The things I worry about never happen.*

ANONYMOUS

WEDNESDAY
Ordinary Time
Week 16 _____

The LORD said to Moses,
"Now I am going to cause food
to rain down from the sky. . . .
[The Israelites] will have meat to eat. . . ."
In the evening
a large flock of quails flew in.

EXODUS 16:4, 12–13

Years ago
National Geographic Magazine
carried this fascinating fact:
"Every year great migrations of quail
wing their way
across the Mediterranean and Red Seas
en route between Europe and Africa.
Even today Bedouin of the Sinai peninsula
catch the exhausted birds
after their long flight over water."
Some Bible readers
think God used ordinary events like this
to feed the Israelites—
in a coincidental way—
in their sojourn across the Sinai desert.

Have I ever experienced God
acting in my life in a coincidental way
through an ordinary event? How?

A coincidence is a small miracle
where God chose to remain anonymous.

HEIDI QUADE

*[The Israelites] came to the desert
of Sinai. There they set up camp
at the foot of Mount Sinai. . . .
On the morning of the third day . . .
the LORD . . . called Moses to the top.*
EXODUS 19:1-2, 16, 20

Modern historians scratch their heads
and ask, "How could a mob of ex-slaves,
with no education and no organization,
change the course of human history?"
The only answer that makes sense
is the one the Israelites themselves gave.
At a mountain in the Sinai desert
they encountered the infinite God
who created heaven and earth.
That incredible encounter changed them
in the most spectacular way imaginable.
They became God's chosen people on earth.
They were never again the same.

What is one way
that my encounter with God
through this program of daily meditation
has changed me?

*Today well lived
makes every yesterday
a dream of happiness
and tomorrow a vision of hope.*
KALIDASA

FRIDAY
Ordinary Time
Week 16 _____

God spoke, and these were his words:
"I am the LORD your God
who brought you out of Egypt,
where you were slaves.
Worship no god but me. . . .
Do not use my name for evil purposes. . . .
Observe the Sabbath."

EXODUS 20: 1-3, 7-8

Many Christians
view the commandments negatively—
as something that restricts them.
The Israelites
viewed the commandments positively—
as something that liberated them.
God's law liberated them
from a life of slavery to sin
for a life of service to God.
Thus the psalmist sings jubilantly,
"[O LORD,] How I love your law!
I think about it all day long. . . .
How sweet is the taste of your
instructions—sweeter even than honey!"
(PSALM 119: 89, 97, 103).

What keeps me from feeling the same
way about God's law as Israel did?

Sin is not hurtful because it is forbidden,
but it is forbidden because it is hurtful.
BENJAMIN FRANKLIN

*[At Mount Sinai] Moses
wrote down all the LORD's commands. . . .
Then he took the book of the covenant,
in which the LORD's commands
were written, and read it aloud
to the people. They said,
"We will obey the LORD and do everything
that he has commanded."* EXODUS 24:4, 7

God's covenant with the Israelites
transformed them from a mob of
ex-slaves into God's chosen people.
It gave them
a new *identity* and a new *destiny*.
Will Herberg says:
"Israel is not a 'natural' nation;
it is, indeed, not a nation at all
like the nations of the world.
It is a supernatural community,
called into being by God
to serve his eternal purposes in history."

In what sense has God given me
a new identity and a new destiny,
not unlike the one he gave Israel?

*Do not desire
to be other than you are,
but desire to be very well what you are.*
SAINT FRANCIS DE SALES

SUNDAY
Ordinary Time
Week 17

One day . . .
one of [Jesus'] disciples said to him,
"Lord, teach us to pray."

LUKE 11:1

Saint Ignatius and some companions
were on an extended journey.
They followed a schedule that
involved stopping at regular intervals
to pray together.
A porter, who had been engaged
to help transport their baggage,
observed this ritual day after day.
He saw the impact it had on them and,
as the days stretched on,
he began to desire to pray with them.
When the saint learned of this desire,
he invited the porter to join them.
It also dawned on Saint Ignatius
that the porter's desire—day after day—
to pray with them was, in itself,
a splendid prayer.

Since starting this program, what is one
helpful thing I've learned about prayer?

Certain thoughts are prayers.
There are moments when,
whatever the attitude of the body,
the soul is on its knees.

VICTOR HUGO

MONDAY
Ordinary Time
Week 17

*[Moses returned to camp and
found the people worshiping a statue.]
He became furious.*

EXODUS 32:19

William Golding's novel *Lord of the Flies*
takes place during World War II.
A plane evacuating 14-year-old boys
from bombed cities in England
crash-lands in the sea.
The pilot and copilot are killed instantly.
But the boys are unharmed and
find safety on a deserted island.
Their life together begins orderly.
But then it deteriorates rapidly,
and the boys start to act like savages.
Something like this
happened to the Israelites
when Moses left them for a while.
A lesson that we might draw
from these two episodes is this:
Sin is never far from our lives.
We need to guard against it—always!

What is the most effective way
I have found to guard against sin?

*The penalty of sin is to face,
not the anger of Jesus,
but the heartbreak in his eyes.*
WILLIAM BARCLAY

TUESDAY
Ordinary Time
Week 17 _____

The LORD
would speak with Moses face-to-face,
just as a man speaks with a friend.
EXODUS 33:11

In *Sadhana*, Anthony de Mello
has an exercise called "The Empty Chair."
He developed it after hearing of an invalid
who had been bedfast for years and
was finding it harder and harder to pray.
One day a friend suggested
placing an empty chair next to the bed
and imagining Jesus sitting on it.
Then the friend suggested talking to
Jesus as they were both talking now.
The sick person tried it
and found it helped immensely.
It was in this personal way
that Moses used to talk to God:
as one close friend
conversing with another.

As I imagine Jesus
sitting opposite me, right now,
what might I say to him?
What might Jesus say to me?

Whoever loses contact with God
lives on the same dead-end street
as an atheist who denies God.
MILTON A. MARCY (adapted)

When Moses
went down from Mount Sinai . . . ,
his face was shining because
he had been speaking with the LORD.

EXODUS 34:29

The Cloud of Unknowing
is an early classic on the spiritual life.
Its author says
that prayerfulness sometimes impacts
one's appearance.
For example, a prayerful person
might radiate a kind of glow.
Saint Elizabeth of Hungary was like this.
A letter dating from the 13th century
says that it was not uncommon to see
"her face shining marvelously
and light coming from her eyes."
Today's reading about the face of Moses
appears to give support
to such observations.
Possibly, it was this phenomenon
that prompted artists to paint haloes
around the heads of saints.

What is one thing that I have observed
about prayerful people?

Whoever prays much by night,
that person's face is fair by day.

ISLAMIC SAYING

THURSDAY
Ordinary Time
Week 17 _____

The first month of the second year
after [the Israelites] left Egypt,
the Tent of the LORD's presence
was set up. . . .
[Moses] took the two stone tablets
and put them in the Covenant Box. . . .
Then he put the Box in the Tent.

EXODUS 40:17, 20–21

In 1967 Israeli soldiers occupied—
for the first time in 1,900 years—
the spot where the Jerusalem Temple
once stood. All that is left now are
huge stone blocks that once formed part
of the spectacular complex.
Today's reading describes
the pioneer model of the Temple.
Tradition says that when the Babylonians
destroyed the Temple, Jeremiah hid
the Covenant Box (Ark of the Covenant)
in a secret cave, whose location has
never been found (2 MACCABEES 2:1–8).

In my imagination, I stand with Jesus
in the Temple, which he called his
Father's house (LUKE 2:49).
What are my thoughts? His thoughts?

How I love your Temple, LORD Almighty!
How I want to be there!

PSALM 84:1

FRIDAY
Ordinary Time
Week 17

[The LORD gave Moses a list of holidays:]
The Passover . . . begins at sunset on the
fourteenth day of the first month.
On the fifteenth day the Festival
of Unleavened Bread begins. . . .
The Festival of Shelters begins on the
fifteenth day of the seventh month.

LEVITICUS 23:5-6, 33-34

Alvin Toffler's book *Future Shock*
deals with the impact
of rapid change in modern society.
He says today, more than ever, we need
a framework for our lives—a pattern
of holidays and rotating seasonal sports.
Without it, we are like someone
in a boat speeding over a trackless sea
with nothing to indicate where we are.
The Israelites weren't concerned about
rapid change, but they knew the value
of a framework for maintaining
regular, quality contact with God.

How is the speed of modern life
impacting my quality contact with God?

Oh, help me, Lord, to take the time
To set all else aside,
That in the secret place of prayer
I may with you abide.

AUTHOR UNKNOWN

SATURDAY
Ordinary Time
Week 17 _____

The LORD spoke to Moses [saying,] . . .
"Set the fiftieth year apart
and proclaim freedom to all. . . .
During this year . . .
anyone who has been sold as a slave
shall return to his family. . . .
The whole year shall be sacred for you."
LEVITICUS 25:1, 10, 12

The fiftieth year
was called the "jubilee year."
The word *jubilee* comes from the Hebrew
word *jubel,* the horn that was blown
to announce the start of the year.
With the start of the year,
all debts were cancelled.
Jesus used the idea of the "jubilee year"
to teach people about the "messianic age,"
which began with his coming (LUKE 4:18).
His coming meant that the spiritual debts
of all peoples were cancelled
and that all people were freed
from the slavery of Satan and sin.

What am I doing with my new freedom?

The fall of the first Adam
was the end of the beginning;
the rise of the second Adam [Jesus]
was the beginning of the end.
S. W. DUFFIELD

SUNDAY
Ordinary Time
Week 18

*[Jesus told a story about a person
who was using his life to acquire wealth,
so that he could enjoy his life later.
Then a voice said,] "You fool! This very
night you will have to give up your life."*

LUKE 12:20

In the 1960s all-pro star Jerry Kramer
wrote a best-seller called *Instant Replay*.
In it he asks this provocative question:
"What's my purpose here on earth
besides playing the silly game
I play every Sunday?"
In the 1980s Kramer wrote a sequel
called *Distant Replay*.
It opens with this provocative question:
"What have I done in my life?"
Kramer answers, regretfully,
that he failed to do
the one thing that he should have done:
pass on "proper values" to his kids.
He writes, "I hadn't done for my children
what my father had done for me."

The story of Kramer invites me to ask,
How well am I doing for my children
what my parents did for me?

*The best use of life is to spend it
for something that outlasts life.*

WILLIAM JAMES

MONDAY
Ordinary Time
Week 18 _____

*[The Israelites complained so bitterly
that Moses said to God,]
"Why have you treated me so badly? . . .
I can't be responsible for all these
people by myself; it's too much for me!"*
                                    NUMBERS 11:11, 14

A woman had a heavy cross to carry.
She went to Saint Peter and said,
"I can no longer carry this heavy cross."
Peter looked at it and said,
"Maybe an angel made a mistake.
What's the cross's serial number?"
The woman said, "001002."
Peter wrote it in his book and said,
"Put the cross over there and see
if you can find one that fits better."
Two hours later the woman returned
with a big smile on her face, saying,
"I've found just the right one."
"Good!" said Peter. "Give me the serial
number and I'll enter it in my book."
The woman said, "Let's see. It's 001002."
Peter said,
"Why, that's the cross you came in with!"

What is the heaviest cross I bear? Why?

*God weeps with us
so that one day we may laugh with God.*
                                    JURGEN MOLTMANN

*Moses was a humble man,
more humble than anyone else on earth.*

NUMBERS 12:3

George Washington Carver began life
as the son of a black slave.
He grew up to get a degree in agriculture
from Iowa State College
and become a great botanist and chemist.
Working at Alabama's Tuskegee University,
Carver revitalized Southern agriculture
by finding new uses for crops.
He once told this story:
"When I was young, I asked God
to tell me the mystery of the Universe.
But God said,
'That knowledge is reserved to me alone.'
So, then, I asked God,
'Tell me the mystery of the peanut.'
Then God said, 'Well, George,
that's more your size.' And he told me."

To what extent
do I tend to upsize my role or posture
in order to impress others? Who and why?

*People hate me
because I am a multifaceted,
talented, wealthy,
and an internationally famous genius.*

Comedian JERRY LEWIS

WEDNESDAY
Ordinary Time
Week 18 _____

All night long
the people cried out in distress.
They complained against Moses and Aaron.

NUMBERS 14:1-2

Father Paul Belliveau is a missionary
from Flushing, New York.
In the 1980s he was pastor
in a Honduran prison camp that housed
over ten thousand Salvadoran refugees.
One day he preached against the hatred
that existed between
the refugees and the Honduran soldiers.
He ended by saying that this was not
the way Jesus taught us to live.
After Mass a young man
grabbed the microphone and shouted,
"Father Paul says we must forgive.
That's easy to say."
Another shouted, "Father Paul doesn't
understand our problem."
Moses and Aaron experienced similar
unjust complaints and hostility.

How well do I keep my composure
when I am unjustly or bitterly attacked?

Speak when you are angry
and you will make the best speech
you will ever regret.

AMBROSE BIERCE

*[The Israelites complained to Moses
about God's failure to give them water.
At God's command, Moses took a stick
and went over to a huge rock.]
Then Moses . . . struck the rock . . . and
a great stream of water gushed out,
and all the people and animals drank.*

NUMBERS 20:11

In the book *Ever Wonder Why?*
Douglas Smith traces the origin
of "clinking" glasses before toasting.
Centuries ago, hosts used parties to
serve poisoned drinks to potential rivals.
To assure a guest that his drink
had not been poisoned, the host
held out his own glass to let the guest
pour some of his drink into it.
If the guest wanted to show the host
that he trusted him, he declined
and simply "clinked" his glass.

What keeps me from "clinking glasses"
with God when I wonder
if God sees and cares about me?

*Courage, brother! do not stumble,
Though the path be dark as night;
There's a star to guide the humble;
Trust in God and do the Right.*

NORMAN MACLEOD

FRIDAY
Ordinary Time
Week 18 _____

[Think of all that God has done for you!]
The LORD your God . . .
chose you, and by his great power
he himself brought you out of Egypt.

DEUTERONOMY 4:34, 37

Henry Ward Beecher
uses this illuminating example.
Suppose someone gave you a dish of sand
mixed with tiny iron filings.
You comb your fingers through the sand,
but you don't see any filings.
Then you take a small magnet
and comb it through the sand.
Suddenly it is covered with filings.
Ungrateful people
are like your fingers combing the sand.
Some Israelites
tended to be terribly ungrateful people.
They combed the "sands of life"
with their fingers and found nothing
for which to give thanks to God.

What is one thing, especially,
for which I ought to give thanks to God
but fail to do so, as I should?

God has two dwellings:
one in heaven and
the other in the meek and grateful heart.

IZAAK WALTON

SATURDAY
Ordinary Time
Week 18

*[Moses said,] "Israel, remember this!
The LORD—and the LORD alone—
is our God. Love the LORD your God
with all your heart, with all your soul,
and with all your strength."*

DEUTERONOMY 6.4-5

In *This Is My God*, Herman Wouk,
best known for his play *The Caine Mutiny*,
says that the Shema
(from which today's reading is taken)
is the first prayer Jews learn and
the last they try to pray before dying.
Wouk says he often wondered if
he would remember it when death came.
Then one day he was on board a ship
in the Pacific when a typhoon struck.
A monstrous wave broke across the ship.
It sent him flying across the deck,
threatening to wash him overboard.
Sure enough, in the midst of the panic,
he remembered the Shema.
At that instant, also, he caught a lifeline
and saved himself from going overboard.

What words am I preparing to pray
at the moment of my death? Why these?

*[Before dying, Jesus prayed,] "Father!
In your hands I place my spirit!"*

LUKE 23:46

SUNDAY
Ordinary Time
Week 19 _____

"Be ready . . .
because the Son of Man will come
at an hour
when you are not expecting him."

LUKE 12:35, 40

Linda Taylor
was putting her three tiny tots to bed.
Suddenly Peggy,
who had just begun kindergarten,
said thoughtfully,
"Mommy, if the world came to an end,
right now . . ."
Linda gulped and said a quick prayer
for guidance.
"Yes, dear," she said, "go on."
Peggy finished her question, saying,
"Would I have to
take my library book back, or
would it be okay to leave it at home?"

Peggy's innocent question
and Jesus' sobering words
invite me to ask,
How ready am I to meet my Maker
at this very moment?

That day which you fear
as being the end of all things
is the birthday of your eternity.

SENECA

*[Some foreigners
were living among the Israelite people.
Moses told the people,]
"Show love for those foreigners, because
you were once foreigners in Egypt."*

DEUTERONOMY 10:19

An old man collapsed on a Brooklyn street
and was taken to Kings County Hospital.
From a blurred address in the man's wallet,
nurses deciphered the name of a marine,
who appeared to be the old man's son.
They put in an emergency call to the camp.
When the marine arrived,
the old man reached out his hand feebly.
The marine took it and held it for the next
four hours—until the man died.
After the man passed away,
the marine asked, "Who was he?"
The nurse replied, "Wasn't he your dad?"
"No," said the marine,
"but I saw he needed a son, so I stayed."

Can I recall a time when a stranger
helped me at great personal expense?
When I helped a stranger?

*None goes his way alone.
All that we send into the lives of others,
Comes back into our own.*

EDWIN MARKHAM

TUESDAY
Ordinary Time
Week 19 ——————————————————

[Moses said to the people,]
"The LORD himself will lead you
and be with you.
He will not fail you or abandon you,
so do not lose courage or be afraid."

DEUTERONOMY 31:8

In his book *Angels,*
Billy Graham says his wife
was born and raised in China.
She still remembers when tigers
roamed the foothills of that country.
One day a Chinese mother
and her two children were walking along.
Suddenly a tiger sprang upon the mother
and sank its claws in her shoulder.
The panic-stricken mother recalled
what a missionary once told her:
"Fear not! Jesus is always ready
to help you in time of trouble."
She cried out, "Jesus help me!"
Instantly, the tiger fled into the hills.

What keeps me from losing heart
when I pray to Jesus for help
but receive no apparent response?

It should be a great comfort to know
that God still has his hands
on the steering wheel of the universe.

E. C. McKENZIE

The LORD said to Moses,
"This is the land that I promised
Abraham, Isaac, and Jacob I would give
to their descendants. I have let you see it,
but I will not let you go there."

DEUTERONOMY 34:4

It is one of the ironies of history
that great leaders
who work so hard for a cause often die
without enjoying the fruit of their labors.
Jesus dedicated his life
to the coming of God's kingdom on earth
but died before seeing it achieved.
Martin Luther King, Jr., dedicated his life
to the "dream" of civil rights
but died before seeing it realized.
John F. Kennedy worked tirelessly
for the sake of America's space program
but died before
seeing an American walk on the moon.

What was one of my childhood dreams?
If I could have one of my dreams come
true, right now, which would it be?
Why this one?

It isn't a calamity
to die with dreams unfulfilled,
but it is a calamity not to dream.

BENJAMIN E. MAYS

THURSDAY
Ordinary Time
Week 19

As the priests stepped into the river,
the water stopped flowing
and piled up. . . .
The flow downstream to the Dead Sea
was completely cut off,
and the people were able to cross over.

JOSHUA 3:15–16

The "crossings"
of the Jordan River and the Red Sea
might be viewed
as opposite sides of the same coin.
The "sea crossing" marks Israel's *exit*
from a land of slavery, while
the "river crossing" marks her *entry*
into a land of freedom.
Christians see these two crossings
reflected in the "baptismal crossing":
exit from a land of slavery to sin and
entry into a land of service to God.

How do I understand Frederich Rest's
statement: "In baptism the direction
is indicated rather than the arrival"?

A part of the act of baptism
in the Church of India
is for the candidates to place
their own hand on their head and say,
"Woe to me if I preach not the Gospel."

E. PAUL HOVEY

"I gave [Abraham] many descendants.
I gave him Isaac, and to Isaac
I gave Jacob and Esau.
I gave Esau the hill country. . . .
I gave you a land."

JOSHUA 24:3-4, 13

A man in the film *The Blues Brothers*
lives in a one-room flat.
It practically sits on a Chicago el track.
When his brother comes to live with him,
the the brother asks,
"How often do the trains go by?"
The man says, "So often
you never notice them."
When something happens often,
after a while we tend not to notice it.
Today's reading makes that point.
If we circled words like *gave,*
we would have at least a dozen circles.
God "gave" Israel so many things—
so often—they took the gifts for granted.

What are some of the things
that God has given me
that I tend to take for granted?

So much has been given me;
I have not time to ponder
over that which has been denied.

HELEN KELLER

SATURDAY
Ordinary Time
Week 19

[The LORD gave Israel many gifts.
In spite of this, many Israelites
still continued to worship false Gods.
Joshua confronted them, saying,]
"Decide today whom you will serve. . . .
As for my family and me,
we will serve the LORD."

JOSHUA 24:15

Lynn went to her doctor for an exam.
After checking her carefully,
her doctor said,
"Lynn, the *best* thing you can do
is to go on a diet, quit smoking,
and start exercising."
Lynn thought a moment and said,
"Doc, I don't deserve the *best*.
What's the second best thing?"
That story illustrates how much
we tend to be like the Israelites.
We know what we should do,
but we don't do it.
We procrastinate and we compromise.
We refuse to "bite the bullet."

What is one area of my life
where I am refusing to "bite the bullet"?
What strategy might I take to change this?

Easy doesn't *do it*.
AL BERNSTEIN

SUNDAY
Ordinary Time
Week 20

[Jesus said,]
"I came to set the earth on fire. . . .
From now on a family of five will be
divided, three against two."

LUKE 12:49, 52

"Calvin and Hobbes" is a cartoon
about a precocious little boy, Calvin,
and his playmate, a talking tiger.
One day Hobbes, the tiger, finds Calvin
sitting under a sign that reads,
"Kick in the butt for one dollar!"
Hobbes asks, "How's business?"
Calvin replies,
"Awful! And I don't know why,
because so many people
need a good kick in the butt!"
Jesus found himself
in a similar situation in his day.
A big part of his mission
was to confront people and get them
to root out the evil in their lives.

Is there an area in my life where I,
perhaps, need a kick to get me
to do something about the evil around me?

There is actually
one thing worse than evil itself,
and that is indifference to evil.

JOSEPH FLETCHER

MONDAY
Ordinary Time
Week 20 _____

The people of Israel sinned. . . .
They stopped worshiping the LORD . . .
and they began to worship other gods. . . .
They bowed down to them
and made the LORD angry.

JUDGES 2:11-12

A columnist asked Cecil B. DeMille,
film director of *The Ten Commandments*,
"What commandment do you think
that people break most today?"
DeMille responded,
"The first, 'Do not bow down to any idol
or worship it' " (EXODUS 20:5).
DeMille added,
"Oh, we don't bow down
before graven images,
but we do worship gods of comfort,
gods of money,
and gods of power."

Which of DeMille's three false gods
am I most tempted to worship?
What is one significant way
that I can guard against making
the same mistake the Israelites did?

The average number of times
that people say "no" to temptation
is about once, weakly.

ANONYMOUS

TUESDAY
Ordinary Time
Week 20

*The LORD ordered [Gideon,] "Go . . .
rescue Israel. . . ." Gideon replied,
"But Lord, how can I rescue Israel?
My clan is the weakest . . .
and I am the least important member. . . ."
The LORD answered, "You can do it
because I will help you."*

JUDGES 6:14–16

A superjet was preparing to land
at Edwards Air Force Base in California.
The pilot pushed the button to lower
the nose gear into landing position,
but it failed to respond.
The pilot did a quick check and traced
the problem to a faulty relay switch.
Looking about for something to bypass
the relay, he found a paper clip,
bent it straight, and then reshaped it
to carry the current around the relay.
It worked and the jet landed safely.

What kind of self-image do I have?
Do I see myself as a "paper clip"
in a world of superjets?
If so, what important thing
is God saying to me in today's reading?

*Whatever your lot in life,
build something on it.*
ANONYMOUS

WEDNESDAY
Ordinary Time
Week 20 _____

*[Jotham told a parable about some trees
that sought a king to rule over them.
The olive tree, the fig tree,
and the grapevine all gave excuses.]
Then all the trees said to the thorn bush,
"You come and be our king."
[And that was their undoing.]*

JUDGES 9:14

Years ago, attorney Louis Rigdon,
who was confined to a wheelchair,
worked for the Department of Justice.
The polling place for his precinct
was located in the basement of a church.
Rigdon paid a cabbie a sizable fee
to drive him to the church,
wheel him to the basement stairway,
and call the voting officials,
who brought him a ballot.
Louis filled it out and returned it.
It was an expensive process,
but he considered his privilege to vote
to be that important.

How responsible am I when it comes
to taking part in governmental affairs?

*The punishment of the wise
who refuse to take part in government
is to live under the rule of the foolish.*

PLATO

THURSDAY
Ordinary Time
Week 20

*[Jephthah was the son of a prostitute.
Forced by society to live as an outcast,
he became the leader of a gang.
Yet when Israel faced a dangerous foe,
it turned to him for help. He accepted.]
Then the spirit of the LORD
came upon Jephthah . . .
and the LORD gave him victory.*

JUDGES 11:29, 32

Frank Harris III
wrote in the *Chicago Tribune:*
"As America's darker citizens,
we have plenty of 'opportunities' to hate.
Hate is, after all, one of the few things
that African-Americans
have had more 'opportunity' to experience
than our white countrymen."
Then Harris turned the corner, saying:
"Hate is blinding, not visionary.
Hate is draining, not fulfilling.
Hate is destructive, not constructive. . . .
That is why we must not hate."

Harris's words and Jephthah's story
invite me to ask,
How do I handle anger and hate?

*Hate is like burning down your house
to get rid of a rat.*

HARRY EMERSON FOSDICK

FRIDAY
Ordinary Time
Week 20

*[Ruth's mother-in-law, Naomi,
was all alone in life.
Ruth promised to care for her
and stay with her always, saying,]
"Wherever you go, I will go;
wherever you live, I will live. . . .
Wherever you die, I will die."*

RUTH 1:16-17

The film *Brian's Song*
celebrates the true story
of a beautiful friendship
between two pro-football players,
Gale Sayers and Brian Piccolo.
Gale is black, Brian was white,
and both played for the Chicago Bears.
When Brian fell fatally ill,
Gale was constantly at his side.
When Brian died,
Gale took a trophy he had just won,
pasted Brian's name on it,
and had it buried with his friend.

Brian's Song and the gospel story
invite me to inventory my friendships.
Am I loyal in good times and bad times?

*A friend is someone
who dances with you in the sunlight
and walks beside you in the shadows.*

ANONYMOUS

Naomi had a relative named Boaz . . .
[who was very kind to Ruth.
Ruth asked him,] "Why should you
be so kind to a foreigner?"
Boaz answered, "I have heard
about everything that you have done
for your mother-in-law."

RUTH 2:1, 10-11

A senior citizen was taking
her daily stroll for her arthritis.
She spotted a five-dollar bill at the edge
of the sidewalk but could not bend over
to pick it up because of her arthritis.
A blind man with a cane came along.
Telling him about her lucky discovery,
she put the tip of his cane on the bill.
He followed down the cane with his hand
and retrieved it.
The two headed for an ice-cream parlor.

That story,
along with the story of Ruth,
shows what a lovely world it could be
if we only tried to make it such.
What keeps me from being
as kind to others as Jesus is to me?

How beautiful a day can be
when kindness touches it.
GEORGE ELLISTON

SUNDAY
Ordinary Time
Week 21 _____

*[Jesus said,] "Do your best
to go in through the narrow door."*

LUKE 13:24

A wealthy woman
was a faithful churchgoer.
Plaques of her many contributions
adorned buildings and objects.
One day she died.
An angel met her at heaven's gate and
escorted her down a wide boulevard
lined with large, lovely mansions.
As they walked, the mansions turned
into houses that got progressively smaller.
Finally, they came to a one-room hut.
"Here you are, madam," said the angel.
"What?" she said indignantly.
"There must be some mistake!"
"I'm sorry," said the angel.
"This was the best we could do
with what you sent us during your life."

What is my main motivation
in donating something to a cause?
In giving something?

*[Jesus said,] "When you give
something . . . do it in such a way
that even your closest friend
will not know about it."*

MATTHEW 6:2-3

[Paul writes,]
We always thank God for you . . .
and always mention you in our prayers.
For we remember
before our God and Father
how you put your faith into practice,
how your love made you work so hard.

1 THESSALONIANS 1:2-3

Seventeen-year-old George Smith
volunteers as a coach and a tutor
at a Detroit youth center.
Sometimes he does his homework
at the center to show the kids
that homework is an important part
of learning.
One of the kids said of George,
"He's almost like a teacher,
maybe a little better,
because he's easy to talk to."

How do I put my faith into practice?
Would people I work with say of me
what the kids said of George?

I look to a time
when brotherhood needs no publicity,
to a time when a brotherhood award
would be as ridiculous as an award
for getting up in the morning.

DANIEL D. MICH

TUESDAY
Ordinary Time
Week 21 ⎯⎯⎯⎯⎯⎯⎯⎯⎯⎯

[Paul writes,]
We were gentle
when we were with you,
like a mother
taking care of her children.

1 THESSALONIANS 2:7

The Wiatomo Caves
are popular New Zealand tourist spots.
One thing that attracts people
is that the domes of the caves
are blanketed with glowworms.
Another thing that attracts people
is the reflection of the glowworms
on the surface of the river
flowing through the caves.
You have to be careful,
however, not to make any noise.
If you do, the glowworms turn off.
Then you see nothing but darkness.
People are like glowworms.
You have to approach them gently,
the way Paul did in today's reading.
If you don't, they turn off.

How could I be more gentle
with the people with whom I work?

Nothing is so strong as gentleness:
nothing so gentle as real strength.

SAINT FRANCIS DE SALES

[Paul writes,]
When we brought you God's message,
you . . . accepted it,
not as man's message but as God's.

1 THESSALONIANS 2:13

Richard Wurmbrand spent
fourteen years in a Communist prison.
He recalls the day when a new prisoner
named Avram arrived. He had been hurt,
and his upper body was in a cast.
When the guards left, Avram felt under
his cast, pulled out a tiny book,
and began reading it.
Soon he realized the other prisoners
were all staring at it.
They hadn't seen a book in years.
It turned out to be a tiny Bible.
Avram had managed to hide it
under his cast at the time of his arrest.
From that day on, that treasured book
was in someone's hands every moment.
The prisoners learned it by heart,
and they discussed it together daily.

What effect has daily meditation had
on my own appreciation of the Bible?

The Gospel is not merely a book—
it is a living power.

NAPOLEON BONAPARTE

THURSDAY
Ordinary Time
Week 21 _____

[Paul writes,] May the Lord
make your love for one another and
for all people grow more and more
and become as great as our love for you.

1 THESSALONIANS 3:12

Fifteen-year-old Scott Ipswitch
began a journal when he got the news
that he was terminally ill with leukemia.
After weeks of being hospitalized,
he was permitted to go home. He wrote:
"I remember the ride home. . . .
The trees, grass, birds, even the sun
seemed to greet me. . . .
For the first time in way over a month,
I was really happy."
Commenting on love, Scott wrote:
"When you are very sick, it helps
to have someone hold your hand,
letting the glowing warmth
of their love for you trickle into you."

How aware am I of the need
to show special love to the sick—
especially sick children?
Who is someone to whom
I ought to show this special love?

To love another person
is to touch the face of God.
Finale of the musical *LES MISERABLES*

FRIDAY
Ordinary Time
Week 21

[Paul writes,]
You learned from us
how you should live
in order to please God. . . .
God wants you to be holy.
1 THESSALONIANS 4.1, 3

In his *Apologia Pro Vita Sua,*
John Henry Newman writes this
about the human conscience:
"It praises, it blames, it promises,
it threatens, it implies a future,
and it witnesses to the unseen.
It is more than man's own self.
The man himself has no power over it,
or only with extreme difficulty;
he may not make it, he cannot destroy it,
he may refuse to use it, but it remains. . . .
Its very existence
throws us out of ourselves,
to go see him in the heights and depths,
whose Voice it is."

One of God's great gifts to help us
achieve holiness is our conscience.
How faithful am I in consulting it
before making important decisions?

Who sacrifices the conscience
burns the picture to obtain the ashes.
CHINESE PROVERB

SATURDAY
Ordinary Time
Week 21 _____

[Paul writes,]
There is no need to write you
about love for your fellow believers.
You yourselves have been taught by God
how you should love one another.

1 THESSALONIANS 4:9

British poet William Dunkerley
also wrote under the name John Oxenham.
One of his poems under this pen name
is especially provocative. It reads:
"To every man there openeth
A way, and ways, and a way.
And the high soul climbs the high way,
And the low soul gropes the low,
And in between, on the misty flats,
The rest drift to and fro.
But to every man there openeth
A high way, and a low.
And every man decideth
The way his soul shall go."

Oxenham's poem and Paul's words
invite me to ask,
Which "way" am I following? Why?

Some men die of shrapnel
And some go down in flames,
But most men perish inch by inch
Playing at little games.

AUTHOR UNKNOWN

[Jesus said,]
"Everyone who makes himself great
will be humbled,
and everyone who humbles himself
will be made great."

LUKE 14:11

Two senior citizens were talking about
the wisdom and the humility
that come with age.
One volunteered,
"When I was young, I was very proud.
My pride caused me more worry!
I was constantly worrying about
what other people thought about me.
When I got older and wiser,
I said to myself,
'I don't care what they think about me.'
And now that I'm even older and wiser,
I realize
they weren't thinking about me at all."

What keeps me from letting others
see me as I truly am? Who is one person
who sees me as I truly am?

We gain more by letting
our real selves to be seen,
than by pretending to be
what we are not.
FRANCOIS DE LA ROCHEFOUCAULD

MONDAY
Ordinary Time
Week 22 ⎯⎯⎯⎯⎯⎯⎯⎯⎯⎯⎯⎯

Those who have died believing in Christ
will rise to life. . . .
And so we will always be with the Lord.
1 THESSALONIANS 4:16-17

Feodor Dostoevski's famous novel
The Brothers Karamazov
has an episode about an old woman
who begins to wonder,
Is there a God? Is there life after death?
When she tells her doubts to Fr. Zossima,
the old priest tells her,
"There's no way to prove these things,
but you can become sure of them."
"How?" she cries.
"Love your neighbor from the heart,"
the priest replies. "The more you love,
the surer you will become about
God's existence and life after death.
The more you love,
the stronger your faith will grow and
the weaker your doubts will become.
This is sure. This has been tried.
This works."

How do I explain Fr. Zossima's advice?
How do I follow it?

Give me faith, Lord,
and let me help others find it.
LEO TOLSTOY

TUESDAY
Ordinary Time
Week 22

[Paul writes,]
The Day of the Lord will come
as a thief comes at night.
When people say,
"Everything is quiet and safe,"
then suddenly destruction will hit them!

1 THESSALONIANS 5:2-3

Mount Vesuvius erupted in A.D. 79.
Its volcanic ash buried people alive—
in the very position they were in
when destruction hit.
The decayed bodies of these people
have left cavities in the hardened ash.
By pouring plaster into these cavities,
archaeologists have reconstructed
many bodies of the victims.
One reconstruction shows a mother
cradling an infant in her arms.
The suddenness of the eruption
reminds us of Paul's warning
of the suddenness of the Lord's return.

What is my instant emotional reaction
when I think of Jesus' Second Coming?

Though my soul may set in darkness,
it will rise in perfect light,
I have loved the stars too fondly
to be fearful of the night.

SARAH WILLIAMS

WEDNESDAY
Ordinary Time
Week 22 _____

[Paul writes,]
The gospel keeps bringing blessings
and is spreading throughout the world,
just as it has among you
ever since the day you first heard
about the grace of God
and came to know it as it really is.

COLOSSIANS 1:6

During World War II, in anticipation of
a harvest festival, a British congregation
decorated its church with ripe corn ears.
That night bombs destroyed the church.
It lay in ruins all winter long.
When spring came, shoots of corn
began to sprout from the rubble.
They grew tall throughout the summer.
When fall came, the congregation
reaped a harvest of golden corn.
The Gospel
is something like the seeds of that corn.
Nothing can keep it from bearing fruit.
The Colossians, in today's reading,
are living witness to this.

What is my response to the charge that
the Gospel is slow in bearing fruit?

Hope is an energy.
It arouses the mind to try every door.

THORNTON WILDER

[Paul writes,] May you be made strong
with all the strength
which comes from his glorious power,
so that you may be able
to endure everything with patience.

COLOSSIANS 1:11-12

A four-year-old
was bombarding her tired father
with questions.
For a while he was very patient.
But now he was near the end of his rope.
"Daddy!" said the four-year-old.
"Yes!" replied her father patiently.
"Daddy, what did you do
at the office today?"
"NOTHING!" he exploded.
After a few seconds of silence
the little girl asked puzzledly, "Well,
how did you know when you were done,
so you could go home?"

With what person in my life, right now,
do I tend to be impatient? Why?
Speak to Jesus about this situation.

If you are patient
in one moment of anger,
you will escape
a hundred days of sorrow.

CHINESE PROVERB

320

FRIDAY
Ordinary Time
Week 22 _____

*Christis the visible likeness
of the invisible God.*

COLOSSIANS 1:15

Adlai Stevenson was fond of this story:
A little girl
was sitting on the kitchen floor.
She had a box of crayons and
was busy drawing a picture of a person.
After a while her mother asked,
"Amy, whose picture are you drawing?"
"It's God's picture," said Amy confidently.
"But, darling," said her mother,
"nobody knows what God looks like."
"They will when I'm finished," said Amy.
Something like that happened in Jesus.
In Jesus, the invisible God
drew a self-portrait in visible flesh.

What amazes me most
about the self-portrait of God in Jesus?

*A God too large
to walk in human shoes
Has outgrown every hope
of human use.
And heavy skeptics
weighted down with doubt
Can never rise
to find what God's about.*

CALVIN MILLER, *The Finale*

*At one time you were far away from God
and were his enemies. . . .
But now, by means of the physical death
of his Son, God has made you his friends.*
COLOSSIANS 1:21-22

Webster's Dictionary defines *atonement*
as "the reconciliation of God and man
through the sacrificial death of Jesus."
The story behind the origin
of the word *atonement* dates to 1526,
when William Tyndale translated
the New Testament into English.
Unable to find an English word to
express the idea of our reconciliation
with God through Jesus' death,
he made one up.
He joined two words: *at* and *onement,*
thus making the word *at-onement,*
or *atonement.*
In other words, by the death of Jesus,
we were made to be "at one" with God.

What are my thoughts as I imagine
myself beneath the cross as Jesus dies?

*From all that dwell below the skies
Let the Creator's praise arise:
Let the Redeemer's name be sung
Through every land, by every tongue.*
ISAAC WATTS

SUNDAY
Ordinary Time
Week 23 _____

*[Jesus said,] "Whoever does not
carry his own cross and come after me
cannot be my disciple."*

LUKE 14:27

Charles Dickens,
author of *The Christmas Carol,*
was the highest-paid writer of his time.
Yet he did not receive a single cent
for the first nine stories he published.
Lawrence Tibbet
became a Metropolitan opera star.
Yet the first time he saw the inside
of the Metropolitan Opera House
was in the standing-room-only section,
because he couldn't afford a seat.
John D. Rockefeller
attained legendary proportions
because of the fortune he amassed.
Yet he started life hoeing potatoes
at four cents an hour.

The stories of people
who began with daily crosses to carry
invite me to ask, What motivates me
to pick up my cross daily and
keep moving forward perseveringly?

*It is no disgrace to start all over.
It is usually an opportunity.*
GEORGE MATTHEW ADAMS

[Paul writes,]
I am happy about my sufferings for you,
for by means of my physical sufferings
I am helping to complete
what still remains of Christ's sufferings
on behalf of his body, the church.

COLOSSIANS 1:24

W. O. Saunders writes of his father,
"I had seen him mend his shoes
and toil for an hour
drawing rusty nails out of old boards
to get the nails
to patch the woodshed or garden fence . . .
that I might wear better shoes than he,
and have the leisure that never was his."
All of us
can recall similar sacrifices
that our own parents made for us.
Yet they endured them gladly.
In a similar way, Paul suffered gladly
for the people to whom he ministered.

How consistently
do I suffer gladly to help those I love?
How consistently do I suffer
to help anyone who simply needs help?

Who helps one's neighbor
helps one's self.

SENECA

TUESDAY
Ordinary Time
Week 23 _____

[Paul writes,]
Since you have accepted Christ Jesus
as Lord, live in union with him.
Keep your roots deep in him,
build your lives on him,
and become stronger in your faith,
as you were taught.
And be filled with thanksgiving.

COLOSSIANS 2:6-7

In his excellent book *Stress of Life,*
stress expert Dr. Hans Selye says
that one of the simplest ways
to reduce stress
is to develop a sense of gratitude.
Selye says that people who focus
on life's blessings invariably experience
contentment and peace,
while people who focus
on life's crosses invariably experience
anxiety and tension.
Paul's recommendation "to be filled with
thanksgiving" is not only good theology
but also good medicine.

For what things, especially, in my life
should I be "filled with thanksgiving"?

Whoever eats food without giving thanks
steals from God.

OLD JEWISH SAYING

[Paul writes,]
You have been raised to life with Christ,
so set your hearts on the things
that are in heaven, where Christ sits
on his throne at the right side of God.

COLOSSIANS 3:1

A young woman bought a beautiful vase
and placed it on a table in her room.
The vase made her see how ugly
the rest of the room really was.
So she cleaned the room and painted it.
Next she washed the windows
and fitted them with new curtains.
Finally she waxed the floor
and put down throw rugs.
Gradually she transformed the room
into something beautiful—
almost as beautiful as the vase.
In a similar way, Paul exhorts
the Colossians to transform their hearts
into something beautiful—as beautiful
as the Christ who now dwells in them.

What is one beautiful thing I might do
to the room of my heart to make it
more like the Christ who inhabits it?

Evil finds a ready home / Where beauty
is despised / And ugliness enthroned.

CALVIN MILLER, *The Finale*

THURSDAY
Ordinary Time
Week 23 _____

You are the people of God; he loved you
and chose you for his own. . . .
Forgive one another
whenever any of you has a complaint
against someone else.
You must forgive one another
just as the Lord has forgiven you.
COLOSSIANS 3:12-13

Father Jenko was one
of many Westerners held hostage
in Lebanon by Muslim extremists
in the 1980s and the 1990s.
After his release, he recalled
some of his experiences in captivity.
One moving experience was
how the attitude of his Muslim guards
softened noticeably when they saw him
making a rosary from string.

Can I recall
of ever having my attitude softened
in a similar way toward someone
whom I disliked or didn't understand?
What does such an experience
tell us about ourselves?

Humanity is never so beautiful
as when praying for forgiveness,
or else forgiving another.
JEAN PAUL RICHTER

[Paul writes,]
I give thanks to Christ Jesus . . .
even though in the past I spoke evil
of him and persecuted and insulted him.
But God was merciful to me
because I did not yet have faith
and so did not know what I was doing.
1 TIMOTHY 1:12-13

One of George Washington's first duties
after taking command of the army
in the Revolutionary War was to expel
Captain John Callender for cowardice
during the Battle of Bunker Hill.
Callender quietly reenlisted as a private.
He went on to fight with such heroism
in the Battle of Long Island
that Washington restored him
to his former rank.
Paul testifies that God treated him
with similar honor.
Paul also went on to become a hero
in his work for God's kingdom.

How heroically am I now working
for God's kingdom—perhaps after
having failed to do so in the past?

Forget your past track record.
Each moment is a new beginning.
AUTHOR UNKNOWN

SATURDAY
Ordinary Time
Week 23 _____

God was merciful to me
in order that Christ Jesus might show
his full patience in dealing with me,
the worst of sinners,
as an example for all those
who would later believe in him.

1 TIMOTHY 1:16

The film *Midnight Express*
concerns an American college student
who was caught smuggling
a small amount of hashish out of Turkey.
Turkish officials decided
to make an example out of him
to show others their impatience
in dealing with offenders.
As the Turkish officials
made an example out of the student,
Jesus made an example out of Paul,
but for the opposite reason:
to teach others his patience
in dealing with offenders.

Why do I imitate the Turkish officials
more than I imitate Jesus
in dealing with offenders?

Patience
is the ability to put up with people
you'd like to put down.

ULRIKE RUFFERT

[Jesus said,] "Suppose one of you
has a hundred sheep and loses one . . .
what does he do? He leaves the other
ninety-nine sheep . . . and goes looking. . . .
When he finds it, he is so happy
that he . . . carries it back home."

LUKE 15:4-5

The parable of the good shepherd
reveals three amazing things
about God's love for us.
First, God's love is *personal*.
God doesn't love us globally,
but individually—each of us
in a special, personal way.
Second, God's love is *unconditional*.
God doesn't love us
only on the condition that we stay good
and do not stray into sin.
God loves us even when we stray—
and to the point of going in search of us.
Finally, God's love is a *rejoicing* love.
God's response upon finding us is
total joy—with no admixture of rebuke.

What dimension of God's love do I,
personally, think is most amazing? Why?

When I go forth to find You,
I find You seeking me.

YEHUDA HALEVI

MONDAY
Ordinary Time
Week 24 _____

[Paul writes,] I urge that petitions . . .
be offered to God for . . . kings
and all others who are in authority.
1 TIMOTHY 2:1-2

British theologian C. S. Lewis
observes correctly
that doctors aren't needed to heal people.
God could heal people directly.
But God decided otherwise—
to make doctors and medicine
the normal channels for healing people.
Similarly, God doesn't need prayer
to move civil leaders to act responsibly.
But God decided otherwise—
to give every citizen the power of prayer
to move civil leaders.
Paul's remarks about prayer remind us
that we must use the power of prayer
to influence civil leadership.
If we don't, God will hold us responsible.

When was the last time I prayed
for a civil leader or for the government?

The tyranny of a prince
in an oligarchy is not so dangerous
to the public welfare
as the apathy of a citizen
in a democracy.
BARON MONTESQUIEU

*[Paul instructs those who aspire
to ministry,] A church leader
must be . . . self-controlled . . .
gentle and peaceful."*

1 TIMOTHY 3:2-3

Airline officials agree
that it's hard to recruit and train people
for the airline industry.
Take stewardesses or stewards.
The good ones have a rare quality
described as "a blend of self-control,
gentleness, and a desire to serve."
Concerning the rarity of this quality
one airline official said, "Today, nobody
wants to be thought of as a servant."
Concerning the importance
of this quality, the same official said,
"When you come right down to it,
service is all we really have to sell."

Paul's words
and those of the airline official
invite me to inventory
my own "self-control, gentleness,
and desire to serve."

*You can never be
what you ought to be
until I am what I ought to be.*

MARTIN LUTHER KING, JR.

WEDNESDAY
Ordinary Time
Week 24

*[Paul writes that
Jesus] appeared in human form . . .
was believed in . . .
and was taken up to heaven.*

1 TIMOTHY 3:16

The Kwa Noi prison camp in Thailand
was a living hell for American
and British soldiers in World War II.
Then one day a couple of prisoners
organized Bible study groups.
The camp situation changed dramatically.
A prisoner recalls the change this way.
He was hobbling back to his shack
one night after a late Bible session.
Suddenly he heard a group of men singing
"Jerusalem the Golden." He wrote later:
"The words of that grand old hymn . . .
made the darkness seem friendly. . . .
The difference between this joyful sound
and the joyless stillness of months past
was the difference between life and death."
It is this kind of difference Jesus made—
and still makes—in our world.

What is one way
Jesus has made a difference in my life?

*I have a great need for Christ;
I have a great Christ for my need.*
CHARLES SPURGEON

[Paul writes,] Be an example
for the believers in your speech,
your conduct, your love, faith, and purity.

1 TIMOTHY 4:12

Just before he died from cancer,
Dr. Lloyd Judd made a series of tapes
to be played when his children
were old enough to appreciate them.
One tape says:
"Are you willing to get out of a warm bed
in the middle of the night when you
desperately need rest, drive 20 miles—
knowing you will not be paid—
to see someone you know can wait
until morning? . . .
If you can answer yes to this,
I feel you are qualified
to start the study of medicine."
Paul held out a similar challenge
to Timothy, his *spiritual son.*
It comes down to this: Be an example
of faith and love to all you meet.

What kind of an example of faith and love
am I to those I meet?

There is a ripple effect in all we do.
What you do touches me;
what I do touches you.

AUTHOR UNKNOWN

FRIDAY
Ordinary Time
Week 24 _____

[Paul warns,] Those who want to get rich
fall into temptation
and are caught in the trap
of many foolish and harmful desires,
which pull them down to ruin
and destruction.   1 TIMOTHY 6:9

The Pit, a novel by Frank Norris,
describes a man
in a huge storage bin used for wheat.
Minutes later, he is buried alive
when unsuspecting workmen
fill the bin with tons of wheat.
The tragic irony of it all is this:
Wheat, meant by God
to be an instrument for preserving life,
becomes an instrument for destroying it.
The story
echoes Paul's point in today's reading.
Wealth, meant by God
to be an instrument for preserving life,
is often the instrument for destroying it.

Is there anything in my life
that God meant to be an instrument of life
that I'm abusing or misusing?

The greatest of all faults
is to be conscious of none.
                          THOMAS CARLYLE

[Paul writes,]
Obey your orders and keep them faithfully
until the Day when our Lord Jesus Christ
will appear.   1 TIMOTHY 6:14

The ancient Greek poet Homer
wrote an epic called *Odyssey.*
In one episode the hero, Ulysses,
meets a sea goddess named Calypso,
who is immortal.
In the course of the meeting,
Calypso, who never met a mortal before,
grows envious of Ulysses. Why?
She realizes that his life is richer
for the simple reason
that his days are numbered.
Therefore his decisions and actions
take on greater urgency and importance.
Not so with her life, and she regrets it.
Paul makes somewhat the same point
in today's reading:
Our decisions and actions are important.

To what extent do I share Calypso's view
of a mortal's life?

When the day of judgment comes,
we shall not be asked what we have read,
but what we have done.

THOMAS A KEMPIS

SUNDAY
Ordinary Time
Week 25 _____

[Jesus told a parable
about a dishonest manager
who learned he was about to be fired.
So he called in his master's debtors
and cut their bills, saying to himself,]
" 'When my job is gone, I shall have friends
who will welcome me in their homes.' "
[Jesus ended the parable, saying,]
"The people of this world are much
more shrewd in handling their affairs
than the people who belong to the light."

LUKE 16:4, 8

Two boys found a purse in a parking lot.
It probably belonged to the elderly lady
who had just driven out of the lot.
The purse contained the lady's name,
her address, and a ten-dollar bill.
One of the boys said, "It's not right
to keep the purse and the money.
But before we return it, let's change
the ten-dollar bill into ten ones."

The stories of the boys and the crooked
manager make me ask, Why am I perhaps
shrewder in handling worldly affairs
than I am in handling heavenly affairs?

Poor eyes limit your sight;
poor vision limits your deeds.

FRANKLIN FIELD

*[The Persian emperor freed the Jews
living in exile in his country, saying,]*
*"Go to Jerusalem and rebuild the Temple
of the LORD, the God of Israel. . . .
If any of his people in exile
need help to return, their neighbors
are to give them this help."*

EZRA 1:3–4

In 1973 a plane of U.S. war prisoners
returned home from Vietnam.
A crowd was waiting to welcome them.
Newsweek described the homecoming:
"While a phalanx of Air Force police
held back the onlookers . . .
the crowd chanted over and over,
'Welcome home, welcome home.' "
The returning Jewish exiles—in today's
reading—received no such welcome.
They came home to a deserted city
and the charred remains of the Temple.

How well do I appreciate
the homecoming God gives me upon my
return after having been held prisoner
by my own sinfulness?

*We wandered across unmarked deserts,
instead of following the road
which the Lord wanted us to travel.*

WISDOM 5:7

TUESDAY
Ordinary Time
Week 25 _____

The Jewish leaders made good progress
with the building of the Temple. . . .
They finished the Temple
on the third day of the month Adar.

EZRA 6:14-15

The returning exiles were heartsick
when they saw the city and the Temple.
Both were destroyed beyond recognition.
Nevertheless they began rebuilding.
It was much harder than anticipated.
Samaritans tried to block their efforts.
Sometimes the people went to work
with a shovel on their right shoulder
and a weapon on their left shoulder.
To add to the hardships,
farm crops failed their first year back.
But led by Ezra and Nehemiah,
they persevered and completed the work
around 450 B.C.
They celebrated by renewing
the covenant and observing the Passover.

What motivates me to hang in there,
day after day,
when everything seems to go wrong?

If you think you can, you can.
And if you think you can't,
you're right.

MARY KAY ASH

[Ezra prayed,] "O God,
I am too ashamed to raise my head....
We, your people, have sinned greatly....
You... have let some of us escape...
and live in safety in this holy place."

EZRA 9:6-9

A woman was strolling
alone one night under the starlit sky.
Suddenly she knelt down and prayed,
"Father, in heaven, I ask you
to give me strength not to offend you,
even in the smallest way."
She had hardly gotten the words out
when a voice said,
"My child, if I granted you that request,
how would I ever be able to show you
the depth of my mercy and forgiveness?"
That story makes the same point
that Ezra makes in his prayer.
God is more willing to forgive us
than we are to ask for forgiveness.

Do I pause nightly to ask God to forgive
my sins of that day? The world's sins?

Ye fearful saints, fresh courage take,
The clouds ye so much dread
Are big with mercy and shall break
In blessings on your head.

WILLIAM COWPER

THURSDAY
Ordinary Time
Week 25 _____

The LORD then gave this message
to the people through the prophet Haggai:
"My people, why should you
be living in well-built houses
while my Temple lies in ruins?
Don't you see what is happening to you?
You have planted much grain,
but have harvested very little. . . .
Can't you see why this has happened?
Now go up into the hills,
get lumber, and rebuild the Temple."

HAGGAI 1:3–8

The people had been freed from exile
for one reason: to return to Jerusalem
to rebuild the Temple.
At first they placed a higher priority
on rebuilding their homes
and making them comfortable.
The task of confronting the people
about misplaced priority fell to Haggai.
Fortunately his words prevailed
and they realigned their priorities.

What is one priority in my life
that might need to be realigned a bit?
What keeps me from doing it?

It is never the wrong time
to do the right thing.
AUTHOR UNKNOWN

*[The LORD spoke again
through the prophet Haggai, saying,]
"When you came out of Egypt, I promised
that I would always be with you.
I am still with you, so do not be afraid."*

HAGGAI 2:5

In early America there were no cars.
Travel was by horse-drawn vehicles.
Roads were often only a pair of tracks
worn into the ground by horses' feet
and the wheels of the vehicles.
Henry David Thoreau
had this image in mind when he wrote:
"I saw a delicate flower
that had grown up two feet high
between the horses' feet
and the wheel track.
An inch more to the right or left
had sealed its fate, or an inch higher.
Yet it lived to flourish,
and never knew the danger it incurred."
In a similar way, God looked after Israel,
protecting her from dangers.

What is one special way
that God has looked after me in my life?

*[God says,] "From the time you were born,
I have helped you. Do not be afraid."*

ISAIAH 44:2

SATURDAY
Ordinary Time
Week 25 _____

Sing and rejoice, O daughter Zion!
See, I am coming to dwell among you,
says the LORD.

ZECHARIAH 2:14 (NAB)

A popular bumper sticker reads,
"Stop the world! I want to get off!"
At times we all feel like that.
We are tempted to say,
"This crazy world is so messed up!
How will we ever restore it
to what God intended it to be?"
Many Jews felt this same way
after the fall of the city of Jerusalem,
the years of exile in Babylon,
and the years of trying to rebuild
the city and the Temple.

When I feel overwhelmed
by the confusion and chaos in the world,
do I make an act of faith
in God's promise in today's reading?
Do I believe, in spite of everything,
that God is still at work in the world?

Our Great Maker
is preparing the world,
in his good time, to become one nation . . .
when armies and navies
will be no longer required.

GENERAL ULYSSES S. GRANT

*[Jesus told a story about a rich man
who ignored the plight of a poor man
whom he passed daily outside his gate.
Both died, and their fates were reversed.
The rich man asked Abraham
to send someone to warn his family,
lest they end up as he did, saying:]*
*" 'If someone were to rise from death
and go to them,
then they would turn from their sins.'
But Abraham said, 'If they will not
listen to Moses and the prophets,
they will not be convinced even if
someone were to rise from death.' "*

LUKE 16:30–31

A new pastor gave a great sermon.
Next Sunday his congregation was filled
with expectation. To their surprise
the pastor repeated the same sermon.
He did the same thing the next Sunday.
When the congregation sent a committee
to him seeking an explanation,
he told them, "I plan to repeat it
until I see you doing something about it."

What keeps me from heeding God's word?

*You can't cross the sea merely by
standing and staring at the water.*
RABINDRANATH TAGORE

MONDAY
Ordinary Time
Week 26 _____

The LORD Almighty
gave this message to Zechariah: . . .
"I will rescue my people from the lands
where they have been taken, and
will bring them back from east and west
to live in Jerusalem. They will be
my people and I will be their God."

ZECHARIAH 8:1, 7-8

Emerald Forest is a movie
about a small boy who gets lost
in the rain forests of South America.
His father never stops searching for him.
Eventually he finds him
living with a tribe of natives.
The movie makes an appropriate parable
of God's concern for the people of Israel.
They had sinned and ended up
far from Jerusalem and the Temple.
When their despair was deepest,
God's love was greatest.
God came to their rescue.

Can I recall a time when I felt deserted—
even forgotten—by God?
It has been said that God is closest to us
at these times. Why?

Our hearts have a God-shaped hole in them
that only God can fill.

AUTHOR UNKNOWN

TUESDAY
Ordinary Time
Week 26

The LORD Almighty says . . .
"In those days ten foreigners
will come to one Jew and say,
'We want to share in your destiny,
because we have heard
that God is with you.' "

ZECHARIAH 8:20, 23

A Brahman priest
told a Christian missionary in India,
"If you Christians were like your book,
you'd conquer India in five years."
The Brahman's point was
that if we lived what the Bible teaches,
we would convert India overnight.
It is this kind of witness
that God talks about in today's reading.
It is the kind of witness
that makes people say to us,
"We want to know more about your God."

Today's reading invites me to ask healing
for whatever keeps me from being
the kind of person
that prompts those around me to say,
"We want to know more about your God."

There are two ways of spreading light:
to be the candle
or the mirror that reflects it.

EDITH WHARTON

WEDNESDAY
Ordinary Time
Week 26 _____

The emperor asked [Nehemiah],
"What is it that you want?"
I prayed to the God of Heaven. . . .
The emperor gave me all I asked for,
because God was with me.

NEHEMIAH 2:4, 8

One form of prayer
that Saint Teresa of Avila used
was simply to stand reverently
and silently in the Lord's presence.
Recommending this method of prayer
to others, she wrote, "Imagine
this Lord himself at your side. . . .
Stay with this good friend
as long as you can. . . . You need not
be concerned about conversing."

How well does this method of prayer
work for me?

Think often on God,
by day, by night, in your business,
and even in your diversions.
God is always near you and with you,
and should not be left alone.
You would think it rude
to leave a friend alone
who came to visit you;
then, must God be neglected?

BROTHER LAWRENCE

THURSDAY
Ordinary Time
Week 26

*All the people raised their arms
in the air and answered,
"Amen! Amen!"
They knelt in worship,
with their faces to the ground.*

NEHEMIAH 8:6

In her book *From Union Square to Rome,*
the great social worker Dorothy Day
describes an episode from her childhood
that had a deep impact on her life:
"I went up to Kathryn's
to call on her to come out to play.
There was no one on the porch. . . .
I burst in. . . . In the front room
Mrs. Barrett was on her knees. . . .
She turned to tell me
that Kathryn and the children
had all gone to the store
and went on with her praying.
And I felt a warm burst of love
toward Mrs. Barrett."

How might I
use my body to help me pray better?
By raising my eyes to heaven
or occasionally speaking out loud?

*When I marched with Dr. King in Selma,
I felt as if my legs were praying.*

RABBI ABRAHAM HESCHEL

FRIDAY
Ordinary Time
Week 26 ⎯⎯⎯⎯⎯⎯⎯⎯⎯⎯

This is the confession you should make:
"The Lord our God is righteous,
but we . . . have disobeyed him.
We did not listen to him."

BARUCH 1:15, 18

In his book *The Taste of New Wine,*
Keith Miller says as a Protestant
he was hesitant to confess to anyone.
He believed confession
should be between God and himself.
At one point, however, Keith discovered
that even if God could forgive him a
certain sin, he couldn't forgive himself.
He anguished over it for months.
Then one day he and a friend
were praying together. He writes:
"In prayer I confessed this sin
aloud to God before this friend.
And within a few days
I could accept God's forgiveness."

What is one sin or action
toward God or another person
that still anguishes me somewhat?
What might I do about it?

When we are honest with another person,
it confirms that we have been honest
with ourselves and with God.

ALCOHOLICS ANONYMOUS MANUAL

Just as you were once determined
to turn away from God,
now turn back and serve him
with ten times more determination.

BARUCH 4:28

In his book *In His Presence,*
Louis Evely says
the worst evil isn't doing evil.
It is doing evil and denying it.
He writes: "Commit straightforward,
clean-cut and undeniable sins
of which you will later be able to repent
with the same sincerity
you used in committing them. . . .
If you are weak enough to sin, do not
be too proud to recognize the fact."

To what extent might Tolstoy's words—
"Everybody thinks of changing humanity,
and nobody thinks of changing himself"—
be true of me?

The disciple asked,
"Does God accept repentance?"
The master replied,
"Do you throw away dirty clothes?"
"No," said disciple.
The master replied,
"Neither will God throw you away."

ANONYMOUS

SUNDAY
Ordinary Time
Week 27 _____

"[Lord!] Make our faith greater."
LUKE 17:5

"The road of life was bright.
It stretched before my sight.
The Lord was at my side
to be my friend and guide.
And so I started out.

"But then the sky grew dark,
and the road grew steep and stark.
Rocks and ruts cut my feet.
My legs grew sore and weak.
I scarce could travel on.

"I turned and cried, 'My Lord!
Why this pain; why this plight?
Why these ruts; why these rocks?
Why this darkness? Where's the light?
I cannot carry on.'

"The Lord replied, 'My child!
Why this fear; why this fright?
Where's your faith? Where's your trust?
Love chose this road for you.
Just trust and travel on.' "
ANONYMOUS

What might I do to build up my faith
and my trust in God's love for me?

Take my hand, precious Lord,
lead me home.
THOMAS A. DORSEY

MONDAY
Ordinary Time
Week 27

*[The LORD called Jonah
to preach to the people of Nineveh.]
Jonah, however,
set out in the opposite direction . . .
to get away from the LORD.*

JONAH 1:3

Psychologist Abraham Maslow says
most of us suffer from a "Jonah complex."
As Jonah fled God's call,
so many of us flee inner calls and dreams.
The reason? We think these things
are beyond our grasp.
Maslow tries to get his point across to
students by asking them, "Which of you
hopes to write the great American novel
or be senator or governor someday?"
The students joke around and laugh.
They think such calls or dreams
are completely beyond their grasp.

What is one inner call or dream
that I thought about but dismissed?

*A blind person's world
is bounded by the limits of touch;
an ignorant person's world,
by the limits of knowledge;
a great person's world,
by the limits of vision.*

E. PAUL HARVEY (slightly adapted)

TUESDAY
Ordinary Time
Week 27 _____

[The LORD spoke to Jonah again.]
"Go to Nineveh, that great city,
and proclaim to the people
the message I have given you."
So Jonah obeyed the LORD and went.

JONAH 3:1-3

A "Peanuts" cartoon
pictures a dejected Charlie Brown.
He is in the dumps
because he failed to help his sister
when the local bully was taunting her.
Linus tries to cheer up Charlie, saying,
"You know what you would do
if the episode happened all over again."
Charlie says, "Yeah, I'd probably
do the same thing again!"
Many of us feel the same way
about our failures and shortcomings.
We've all but given up trying to change.
Today's reading suggests otherwise.
God is a persistent lover,
who keeps calling and gracing us.

How convinced am I that if I keep trying,
God's grace will eventually win out
over my human weakness.

It takes twenty years
to make an overnight success.

Comedian EDDIE CANTOR

*[Jonah grew angry when a plant
he was fond of died suddenly.
God said to him,] "You feel sorry for it!
How much more, then, should I have pity
on Nineveh. . . . After all, it has
more than 120,000 innocent children."*

JONAH 4:10-11

A child on a school bus swallowed a
crayon that lodged in his windpipe.
The bus driver tried to flag a motorist
to rush the boy to a hospital,
but no one would pull over to help.
Finally the desperate driver
forced a motorist to stop by blocking
the traffic lane with his own body.
But the motorist still refused to help,
saying he would be late for work.
When the driver finally got the child
to a hospital, it was too late.
Like Jonah,
people get so preoccupied
with their problems that they can't see
the bigger ones other people have.

How hard is it for me to see beyond
my world and my own troubles?

*When I dig others out of trouble,
I find a place to bury my own.*

AUTHOR UNKNOWN

THURSDAY
Ordinary Time
Week 27 _____

[The LORD says,]
"On the day when I act . . .
people will see the difference
between what happens . . . to the person
who serves me and the one who does not."

MALACHI 3:17-18

A "Peanuts" cartoon
shows Lucy holding a music box
up to her ear and listening attentively.
After a few seconds
she turns to Charlie Brown and explains,
"I always like to begin my day
listening to good music."
Obviously unimpressed, Charlie says,
"I'm not concerned how my day begins.
It's how it ends that bothers me."
The prophet Malachi
would agree with Charlie.
He warns evildoers that the LORD
will hold them accountable in the end
for the way they have served—
or not served—the LORD.

How foresighted am I when it comes
to the conduct in my own life on earth?

It is not only what we do,
but also what we do not do,
for which we are held accountable.

MOLIERE

Blow the trumpet; sound the alarm. . . .
The day of the LORD is coming soon.

JOEL 2:1

More than 1,500 people lost their lives
when the *Titanic* sank in the Atlantic
on April 15, 1912.
Not long ago a magazine asked,
"If you had been on the *Titanic*
when it was sinking, would you have busied
yourself rearranging the deck chairs?"
At first the question seems ridiculous,
but then the point dawns.
The world is faced with unprecedented
problems that, if left unchecked,
could sink it.
Yet we ignore them and go about
"rearranging the deck chairs."
Today's reading is a warning
not only to the people of Malachi's time
but also to the people of our time.

To what extent,
in my own personal life,
might I be "rearranging deck chairs"?

There are three classes of people:
those who make things happen,
those who watch things happen,
those who have no idea what's happening.

ANONYMOUS

SATURDAY
Ordinary Time
Week 27 _____

*[The LORD promised to restore Israel
to its former glory, saying,]
"Then shall you know that I, the LORD,
am your God."*   JOEL 4:17 (NAB)

A saintly woman was severely tempted
by the devil.
She prayed and prayed for help,
but God didn't seem to hear her prayers.
At last the temptation subsided.
When God appeared, the lady asked,
"God, where were you
when the devil was tempting me?"
God replied,
"Where I am now—at your side."
When trampled underfoot
by hostile nations,
Israel also felt abandoned by God.
Israel also asked, "God, where are you?"
But the prophet Joel reassured Israel
that God is "at your side."

When was the last time
that I felt abandoned by God? Why?

*Do not be afraid—I am with you!
I am your God—let nothing terrify you!
I will make you strong and help you;
I will protect you and save you.*
                                   ISAIAH 41:10

SUNDAY
Ordinary Time
Week 28

[Ten lepers shouted to Jesus,]
"Have pity on us!" [Jesus shouted back,]
"Go and let the priests examine you."
On the way they were made clean.
[But only one returned to thank Jesus.]
LUKE 17:13-14

Germaine Gardner was born with
one eye, no nose, and a misshapen face.
Doctors said he would be a vegetable.
His mother wanted him to die.
Now, at four years old, he was sitting
in the lobby of Medical City Dallas,
playing a "thank-you" piano concert
for 200 hospital employees.
His musical talent was discovered
accidentally when he was still a baby.
He now has a memorized repertoire
of nearly 200 classical compositions
(Germaine calls popular music "junk")
and has played with
world-famous pianist Stevie Wonder.

The four-year-old's "thank-you" concert
makes me ask, How grateful am I
for what I have, and how do I show it?

Happy are they who grieve not
for what they have not,
but give thanks for what they do have.
AUTHOR UNKNOWN

MONDAY
Ordinary Time
Week 28 _____

[Paul writes,]
God gave me the privilege of
being an apostle for the sake of Christ,
in order to lead people of all nations
to believe.   ROMANS 1:5

There's a delightful story
about a old man who saw a sparrow
lying on its back,
holding its legs toward the sky.
The old man asked the tiny sparrow,
"Why are you lying like that?"
The sparrow replied, "We're told
that the sky is going to fall today."
The old man laughed uproariously and
said to the sparrow, "Do you think
your toothpick legs can hold up the sky?"
The tiny sparrow said,
"No, but I must do what I can."

When it comes to making known
the Good News of Jesus,
do I follow the defeatist's philosophy
and say, "What can a person like me do?"
Or do I follow the sparrow's philosophy
and say, "I must do what I can"?

The only failure that is truly tragic—
not to try and fail, but to fail to try.
                    ANONYMOUS

Ever since God created the world,
his invisible qualities, both
his eternal power and his divine nature,
have been clearly seen; they are perceived
in the things that God has made.

ROMANS 1:20

A Western scholar
was bragging to an Arab
about the power of the telescope.
The Arab listened carefully.
When the scholar stopped talking,
the Arab said to him,
"You Westerners see millions of stars
and nothing else.
We Arabs see only a few stars and God."

Am I one of those Westerners who see
"millions of stars and nothing else"?
How might I learn to see, more clearly,
beyond these stars to their Creator?

The sun is so large that,
if it were hollow, it could contain
more than one million worlds
of the size of our earth.
There are stars in space so large
that they could easily
hold 500 million suns
of the size of ours.

MORRIS MANDELL

WEDNESDAY
Ordinary Time
Week 28

*When you judge others and
then do the same thing which they do,
you condemn yourself. . . . Do you think
you will escape God's judgment?*

ROMANS 2:1, 3

A humorist said something like this:
"If I strive for money, I'm greedy;
if I don't, I'm lazy.
If I save my money, I'm miserly;
if I don't, I'm irresponsible.
If I'm generous with money, I'm foolish;
if I'm not, I'm selfish."
The humorist had a point.
No matter what we do,
someone is ready to pass judgment on us.
So what do we do?
One woman replied this way:
"Be at peace with whatever you do
and ignore those who pass judgment;
any fool can do it and most fools do."

How prone am I
to pass judgment on the people
with whom I live or work? Why?

*When you meet someone,
you judge them by their clothes;
when you leave them,
you judge them by their heart.*

RUSSIAN PROVERB

*Everyone has sinned and is far away
from God's saving presence.
But by the free gift of God's grace
all are put right with him
through Christ Jesus. . . . God offered him,
so that by his sacrificial death
he should become the means
by which people's sins are forgiven.*

ROMANS 3:23–26

An anonymous poet wrote this prayer:
"I try to forget you, Lord;
but you keep stalking me. Why?
I guess that's what love is all about.
If you can love like that, Lord,
then you must be God.
And because you are God,
you have the power
to reach me, to touch me, to change me,
to make me over.
Lord, never give up on me,
even should I give up on you."

How honestly can I pray this prayer?

*Give me the strength
to meet each day with quiet will.
Give me the faith
to know Thou art
my shepherd still.*

HEBREW UNION HOME PRAYER BOOK

FRIDAY
Ordinary Time
Week 28

*"Happy are those whose wrongs
are forgiven, whose sins . . .
the Lord will not keep account of!"*

ROMANS 4:7–8

A young woman with a sinful past
went down to the ocean.
She thought her life was a failure
and planned to end it by swimming out
beyond the point of return.
As she walked along the beach
sobbing her good-byes to the world,
an inner voice told her to look back.
When she did, she saw the surf
erasing all trace of her footprints.
Then the voice said, "So has
my love and mercy erased all your past.
I am calling on you to live and love,
not die."

JOHN POWELL, S.J., *He Touched Me*

What are some things that God's love
and mercy have erased from my past?

*The quality of mercy is not strain'd;
It droppeth as gentle rain from heaven
Upon the place beneath.
It is twice blest:
It blesseth him that gives
and him that takes.*

WILLIAM SHAKESPEARE

When God promised Abraham
and his descendants that the world
would belong to him, he did so,
not because Abraham obeyed the Law,
but because he believed. . . .
And so the promise was based on faith,
in order that the promise
should be guaranteed as God's free gift
to all of Abraham's descendants.

ROMANS 4:13, 16

A woman grew more and more depressed
as she meditated on Jesus' teaching
about giving to others (LUKE 6:37-38).
An angel came to comfort her, asking,
"Why are you sad, lovely child of grace?"
The woman replied, through tear filled eyes,
"Because of what Jesus says about giving.
Does the Master mean I must give
again and again, without stopping?"
"Oh, heaven's no!" said the angel.
"The Master asks you to give to others
only as long as God keeps giving to you."

What was my last gift to someone?
What was my reason for giving it?

When we die
we clutch in our hands only that
which we gave away in our lifetime.

JEAN JACQUES ROUSSEAU

SUNDAY
Ordinary Time
Week 29

*Jesus told his disciples a parable
to teach them that they should always
pray and never become discouraged.
[It concerned a widow
who kept badgering a judge to help her.
He finally gave in and helped her.]*

LUKE 18:1

Dan Reuttiger stood 5 feet 6½ inches
and had "the physique of an inner tube."
He also had the "corny dream"
of playing football at Notre Dame.
Twice Dan applied to Notre Dame,
and twice the school turned him down.
He spent most of one night praying
at the grotto of Our Lady on campus,
and the third time they admitted him.
Incredibly, he made the team
and went on to hear 59,075 fans scream
at the final game of the season,
"Reuttie! Reuttie! Reuttie!"
But there's even more to his story.
Reuttie's "corny dream" was picked up
by Hollywood and made into a movie.

To what extent am I as tenacious as
"Reuttie" and the widow in the gospel?

*God, give me the determination and
tenacity of a weed.*

MRS. LEON WALTERS

MONDAY
Ordinary Time
Week 29

*[Abraham's] faith did not leave him,
and he did not doubt God's promise;
his faith filled him with power,
and he gave praise to God.*

ROMANS 4:20

British writer and television celebrity
Malcolm Muggeridge
entered the Catholic Church in 1982.
In an interview in the *U.S. Catholic,*
he describes a milestone
in his long journey of faith. He says:
"It was while in the Holy Land
for the purpose of making
three BBC television programs
on the New Testament that a curious,
almost magical certainty seized me
about Jesus' birth, ministry,
and crucifixion."
Like Abraham, once Muggeridge
embraced the gift of faith,
he was certain that he was home.

To what event or person, especially,
do I owe my gift of faith?

*Faith will not be restored to the West
because people believe it to be useful.
It will return
only when they find that it is true.*

BARBARA WARD

TUESDAY
Ordinary Time
Week 29 _____

Sin came into the world through one man,
and his sin brought death with it. . . .
So then, as the one sin condemned all . . .
in the same way the one righteous act
sets all . . . free and gives them life.

ROMANS 5:12, 18

John Steinbeck
wrote in his novel *East of Eden:*
"Two stories haunted us
and followed us from the beginning . . .
the story of original sin and
the story of Cain and Abel.
And I don't understand them at all,
but I feel them in myself."
Each of us carries within our person
the result of the first sin.
We feel in ourselves a pull toward evil.
This should not discourage us.
For even though the pull is great,
the grace of Christ is greater still.

How do I feel Steinbeck's two stories
impacting my life right now?

As the grave grows nearer
my theology
is growing strangely simple,
and it begins and ends with Christ
as the only savior of the lost.

HENRY BENJAMIN WHIPPLE

WEDNESDAY
Ordinary Time
Week 29

*Sin must
no longer rule in your mortal bodies,
so that you obey the desires
of your natural self.*

ROMANS 6:12

A local high school choir was singing,
with high emotion and strained voices,
"Carry Me Back to Old Virginia."
A lady in the audience began to weep.
The person next to her said tenderly,
"Are you a Virginian?"
"No," said the lady, "I'm a musician."
Sometimes God must feel
the way the woman felt.
God must weep
at the way we're singing the song of life,
compared to the way
that God intended it to be sung.

In what way am I doing a fairly good job
of singing God's song of life?
In what way might I improve upon
how I am singing it?

*The LORD looks down from heaven . . .
to see if there are any who are wise. . . .
But they have all gone wrong;
they are all equally bad.
Not one of them does what is right.*

PSALM 14:2-3

THURSDAY
Ordinary Time
Week 29

At one time
you surrendered yourselves entirely
as slaves . . . for wicked purposes.
In the same way you must now
surrender yourselves entirely
as slaves . . . for holy purposes.

ROMANS 6:19

"In Downey, California, a man . . .
went through the prime-rib line
seven times at Marmac's,
a restaurant that provides
an unlimited amount of roast beef. . . .
He wound up in a hospital,
having his stomach pumped out.
But less than a week later,
he was back in the beef line."

TIME magazine

It is this kind of a slavery to sin
that Paul refers to in today's reading.
Now Paul urges the Romans
to let Jesus reign in their hearts
just as fully as sin once did.

How fully does Jesus reign in my heart?

Ring in the valiant man and free,
The larger heart, the kindlier hand;
Ring out the darkness of the land;
Ring in the Christ that is to be.

ALFRED LORD TENNYSON

FRIDAY
Ordinary Time
Week 29

I don't do the good I want to do;
instead, I do the evil
that I do not want to do.

ROMANS 7:19

A traveling salesman
was assigned to work in a rural area.
One day he came upon a farmer
sitting in a rocking chair
on the porch of a rundown house.
After introducing himself,
he launched eloquently into his pitch:
"Sir, I have a remarkable book for you.
It describes how you can farm your land
ten times better than you're doing now."
The farmer continued to rock.
Then, after a long pause, he said,
"Young fella! I know how to farm
ten times better than I'm doing now.
My problem is doing it."

Do I fail more by commission
(doing what I ought not to do)
or more by omission
(not doing what I ought to do)?

Who will rescue me from this body
that is taking me to death?
Thanks be to God, who does this
through our Lord Jesus Christ!

ROMANS 7:24-25

SATURDAY
Ordinary Time
Week 29 _____

If the Spirit of God,
who raised Jesus from death, lives in you,
then he who raised Christ from death
will also give life to your mortal bodies
by the presence of his Spirit in you.

ROMANS 8:11

In *The Taste of New Wine,*
Keith Miller says his spirituality
took a giant leap toward maturity
when he ceased being concerned about
not always feeling God's presence—
especially in time of prayer. He writes:
"I realized that so much of my life
I had been a spiritual sensualist,
always wanting to feel God's presence
in my prayers
and being depressed when I didn't. . . .
And I realized a strange thing:
that if a person in his praying
has the *feeling,* he doesn't need the *faith.*"

How do I interpret Miller's last sentence?

Sometimes we are "gifted" in prayer
with the tenderness of God's presence.
When this happens,
we simply savor the "gift" gently,
allowing God to hold us lovingly
as a loving mother holds her child.

ANONYMOUS

[Jesus said,]
"Everyone who makes himself great
will be humbled, and everyone
who humbles himself will be made great."

LUKE 18:14

A newly commissioned colonel
had just moved into his office.
A private entered with a tool box.
To impress the private, the colonel said,
"Be with you in a minute, soldier!
I got a phone call as you were knocking."
Picking up his phone, the colonel said,
"General, it's you! How can I help you?"
A dramatic pause followed.
Then the colonel said, "No problem.
I'll phone Washington
and talk to the president about it."
Putting down the phone,
the colonel said to the private,
"Now, what can I do for you?"
The private shuffled his feet and said,
sheepishly, "Oh, just a little thing, sir.
They just sent me to hook up your phone."

How prone am I to name-drop or brag?
What seems to be the reason for it?

He who stays not in his littleness
loses his greatness.

SAINT FRANCIS DE SALES

MONDAY
Ordinary Time
Week 30 _____

If we share Christ's suffering,
we will also share his glory.
ROMANS 8:17

Time magazine reported on a priest
who spent years in a Romanian prison.
He was kept in total darkness
in an underground cell
next to an open sewer into which toilets
from several upper floors drained.
The stench was overwhelming.
He slept on two three-foot boards
on a damp floor. Rats scurried about him.
The priest said later,
"It pleased God to fill my cell with . . .
part of his glory. . . .
There is a part of the living God
which is only known to those who are . . . .
in darkness and in chains. . . .
God's happiness rests longer on those
who have not light's distraction."

How badly do I want to see God's glory?
How ready am I to sit in the dark to do so?

You do not have to sit outside
in the dark. If, however,
you want to look at the stars,
you will find that darkness is required.
The stars neither require it
nor demand it.   ANNIE DILLARD

What we suffer at this present time
cannot be compared at all
with the glory
that is going to be revealed to us.

ROMANS 8:18

The link between success in sports
and suffering is a popular film theme:
Rocky (boxing), *Chariots of Fire* (track),
Vision Quest (wrestling), and
The Karate Kid (karate).
Each of these sports movies dramatizes
how suffering is the price
an athlete willingly pays for success.
The same is true of other endeavors:
Paper Chase (law), *Fame* (theater), and
St. Elsewhere (medicine).
In other words, the popular maxim
"No pain, no gain" holds true
not only in dojos and dressing rooms,
but also in offices and operating rooms.
The maxim also holds true
for the spiritual life, as Paul tells us.

How ready am I to accept pain now
in order to share God's glory later?

Lord, I do not ask
that I never be afflicted, but only
that you never abandon me in affliction.

SAINT BERNADETTE SOUBIROUS

WEDNESDAY
Ordinary Time
Week 30 _____

The Spirit also comes to help us,
weak as we are.

ROMANS 8:26

A car accident left Peter Saraceno
motionless, speechless, hopeless.
His fiancée, Linda Fraschalla,
quit her job to nurse him during a coma
that lasted three and a half months.
She talked to him, even though
he gave no sign of hearing her.
She massaged his limbs—prayed for him.
Then one day she saw his eyebrow move.
Next she heard him say his first word.
Two years later Linda steadied Peter
as he walked with her down the aisle
of Our Lady of Pompeii at their wedding.
What Linda did for Peter,
the Holy Spirit does for each of us:
helps us that we may help others.

Where do I experience the Spirit's help
most in my life, right now?

As soil can produce nothing for us
unless energized
by the power of the sun,
so we can produce nothing for God
unless energized
by the power of the Spirit.

ANONYMOUS

*Nothing . . . will ever be able
to separate us from the love of God.*
ROMANS 8:39

A young mother used to hurry home
and spend her lunch hour with Marion,
her child, who was staying next door.
But when she left again after lunch,
Marion grew hysterical.
One day the mother stopped coming.
Years later, Marion learned
that her mother still came each noon,
sat at the window, watched her play,
and longed to hold her close—
especially when Marion fell or cried.
But for the child's good, she didn't.
Looking back on it now, Marion knows
why her mother stopped coming.
It was because she loved her:
it was for her own good.
This story explains why God sometimes
seems to withdraw from us—
even for long periods—in our prayer life.
It's for our good: to deepen our faith.

How do I pray when God seems distant?

*As a deer
longs for a stream of cool water,
so I long for you, O God.*
PSALM 42:1

FRIDAY
Ordinary Time
Week 30 _____

[Concerning Jews who rejected Jesus,
Paul writes,] How great is my sorrow,
how endless the pain in my heart
for my people, my own flesh and blood!

ROMANS 9:2–3

An old preacher
was working long into the night
on a sermon for his tiny congregation.
His wife challenged him
on the wisdom of spending so much time
for so few people.
The old man was unmoved by her words
and kept right on working.
The old preacher's flock
was far more important to him
than any sleep or rest.
Paul possessed the same readiness
to sacrifice generously
for his Jewish brothers and sisters.
He was ready to endure any hardship
to be able to share with them
the same love and peace
Jesus had shared with him.

How do I account for the generosity
that motivates people like Paul?

It is not enough for me to love God
if my neighbor does not love God.

SAINT VINCENT DE PAUL

[Paul asks,]
Did God reject [God's] own people? . . .
When the Jews stumbled,
did they fall to their ruin?
By no means! . . . God does not change.

ROMANS 11:1, 11, 29

Baseball fans remember Jimmy Piersall,
who played for the Red Sox
in the early 1950s.
They also remember his book,
Fear Strikes Out,
the bittersweet story of his life.
In his rookie year
he suffered a nervous breakdown and
was committed to a mental hospital.
During this trying year his wife, Mary,
was constantly at his side—
loving, encouraging, helping him.
Commenting on her touching fidelity,
Albert Cylwicki observes,
"Mary's fidelity to Jim
is a reflection of God's fidelity to us."

How well do I reflect God's fidelity?

It is possible
to give without loving,
but it is impossible
to love without giving.

RICHARD BROUNSTEIN

SUNDAY
Ordinary Time
Week 31 _____

[Jesus said,]
"The Son of Man came
to seek and to save the lost."
LUKE 19:10

Columnist Scott Bennett
tells this true story about a man
whom he identifies only as "Michael."
His marriage was ending, he had no job,
his father had died a month earlier,
and his car had just been repossessed.
One night, in a desperate cry of help,
Michael "lifted his face to the stars."
Then the incredible happened! He said:
"I felt I was one with . . .
call it God, call it creation . . .
I don't know. I do know I felt a peace
I have never known before, or since.
A power and a purpose
were revealed to me that night
I cannot put into words.
But I have never doubted again
that life is precious and has a purpose."

Was there a time when I experienced
something akin to what Michael did?

"Do not be afraid or discouraged
for I, the LORD your God,
am with you wherever you go."
JOSHUA 1:9

MONDAY
Ordinary Time
Week 31

How great are God's riches!
How deep
are his wisdom and knowledge!
Who can explain his decisions?
Who can understand his ways?

ROMANS 11:33

British Theologian Frank Sheed
writes in his book *Theology and Sanity:*
"There is something
marvelously inviting to the mind
in an Infinite Being
of whom we can know something,
but whom we cannot wholly know;
in the knowledge of whom we can grow,
yet the truth of whose being
we can never exhaust;
we shall never have to throw God away
like an unsolved crossword puzzle."

How do I visualize God
when I meditate or pray to God?
Why do I tend to visualize God
in this manner?

Time doesn't enfold God;
space can't hold God.
Intelligence can't grasp God.
Imagination can't conceive God.
Absolutely nothing is like God.

ABDALLAH IBN TUMART

TUESDAY
Ordinary Time
Week 31

[Paul exhorts the Romans,]
Work hard and do not be lazy.
Serve the Lord
with a heart full of devotion.
Let your hope keep you joyful.
ROMANS 12:11-12

Golfer Chi Chi Rodriquez
has won over 20 PGA tournaments.
He says, with justifiable pride,
that he began his career
not at a New York country club,
driving round balls with a two iron,
but in a Puerto Rican cane field,
"driving oxen with a broomstick."
Chi Chi explains:
"I would walk behind an ox,
guiding him with a broomstick.
For $1 a day
I worked eight hours straight,
with no food breaks."

With what kind of diligence
and devotion do I carry out my work?
What is my chief motivation
for doing the best job I can?

Every job is a self-portrait
of the person who did it.
Autograph your work with quality.
AUTHOR UNKNOWN

The only obligation you have
is to love one another.
Whoever does this has obeyed the Law.
ROMANS 13:8

Long before expressways and motels
were commonplace,
a cloudburst stranded a newlywed couple
on a country road.
They walked to a nearby farmhouse,
where an elderly couple invited them in
and gave them a room for the night.
Next morning the newlyweds rose early
and prepared to leave quietly,
without disturbing the elderly couple.
When they reached the living room,
they found the couple asleep in chairs.
Their young-at-heart hosts
had given them their only bedroom.

How graciously do I share with others—
even with "strangers"?

There are three kinds of giving:
grudge giving,
duty giving, and
thanks giving.
Grudge giving says, "I hate to";
duty giving says, "I ought to";
thanks giving says, "I want to."
ROBERT RODENMAYER (slightly adapted)

All of us
will stand before God to be judged. . . .
Every one of us, then,
will have to give an account.

ROMANS 14:10, 12

A line was forming
behind an elderly man who was slow
in using an automatic teller machine.
Someone shouted impatiently,
"Hey, pop! I don't have all day like you!"
The elderly man was visibly shaken.
Just then
a young women stepped out of line,
went up to the elderly man, and said,
"Can I help, sir?" "Please do," he said.
"It's my first time using the machine,
and I don't think I'm doing it right."

When difficult situations develop,
do I tend to respond
like the person who yelled,
or like the young woman who helped?

Those who follow
that part of themselves that is great
are great people;
those who follow
that part of themselves that is small
are small people.

CHINESE PROVERB

*My ambition has always been
to proclaim the Good News in places
where Christ has not been heard of.*
ROMANS 15:20

Television's Phil Donohue
says that commitment is made up
of three stages.
First, there is the *fun* stage.
That's when I say, "I love doing this.
Why didn't I get involved sooner?"
Then there's the *intolerant* stage.
That's when I say,
"Anyone who's not involved
isn't really Christian!"
Finally, there's the *reality* stage.
That's when I realize my involvement
will probably make only a slight dent
in the war against evil.
It's at that stage that saints are made.

At what stage am I?
What motivates me to stay involved?

*The happiest people in the world
are those
who have found the life task
to which they have been called. . . .
[And the unhappiest] are those
who have not even begun to search.*
ROBERT C. LESLIE

SATURDAY
Ordinary Time
Week 31 _____

[Paul exhorts Christians to show love and
affection toward one another, saying,]
Greet one another with a . . . kiss.

ROMANS 16:16

Psychologist Rollo May
has this provocative passage
in his book *Man in Search of Himself:*
"Dr. Walter Canon has shown
in his study of 'voodoo death' that
primitive people may be literally killed
by being psychologically isolated
from the community.
There have been cases of natives
who, when socially ostracized
and treated by their tribes
as though they did not exist,
have actually withered and died."

What are some marks of affection
that I can show simply and sincerely
to some around me who truly need it?

We have learned
to fly in the air like birds
and swim in the sea like fish.
But we have not learned
the simple act of living together
as brothers [and sisters].

MARTIN LUTHER KING, JR.
(accepting the Nobel prize)

[Asked about the afterlife, Jesus said,]
"Moses clearly proves that the dead
are raised. . . . He speaks of the Lord
as . . . the God of the living."

LUKE 20:37-38

A little girl bounced excitedly
up the airport ramp to board a plane.
"Where are you going?" her mother asked.
Without missing a bounce, she said,
"To Granny's! To Granny's! To Granny's!"
The girl's answer helps to illustrate
Jesus' point about the afterlife.
We should think of it not so much
as being in a *place* as being with a *person*.
Jesus says to Mary Magdalene,
"Tell them [the disciples]
that I am returning
to . . . my God and their God" (JOHN 20:17).

From strictly a natural point of view,
why does an afterlife seem logical?

From the voiceless lips
of the unreplying dead
there comes no word.
But in the night of Death,
Hope sees a star,
and listening Love can hear
the rustle of a wing.

ROBERT GREEN INGERSOLL

MONDAY
Ordinary Time
Week 32 _____

The Lord's spirit fills the entire world,
and holds everything in it together.

WISDOM 1:7

Saint Francis used to address the sun
and the moon as "brother" and "sister."
We think this strange,
because we don't think of them this way.
Schooled in Western science, we are
trained to see how different things are.
Schooled in another science,
he was trained to see how alike they are.
He saw how all came from God's hand
and is held together by God's power.
All of creation is a product of God's love
and a part of God's extended family.
And so, Francis addressed created things
as "brother" and "sister."

What kinship do I feel
with the rest of God's creation?
What part of God's creation
speaks to me most about our Creator?
What does it say to me?

[God's] plan, which God will complete
when the time is right,
is to bring all creation together,
everything in heaven and on earth,
with Christ as head.

EPHESIANS 1:10

Those who have put their trust in God
will come to understand
the truth of his ways.
Those who have been faithful
will live with him in his love.

WISDOM 3:9

During a visit to Peru in the 1980s,
Pope John Paul II was deeply moved
by a spokesperson for the poor who said:
"We are hungry, we live in misery,
we are sick and out of work.
Our women give birth in tuberculosis,
our infants die, our children grow weak
and without a future.
But despite this
we believe in the God of life.
We have walked
with the Church and in the Church,
and it has helped us . . . to live in dignity
as children of God
and brothers [and sisters] of Christ."

If the pope asked me to respond to the
spokesperson, what might I say and why?

The world
and everything in it that people desire
is passing away;
but [whoever] does the will of God
lives forever.

1 JOHN 2:17

WEDNESDAY
Ordinary Time
Week 32 _____

I write these words,
so that you may know how to act wisely
and avoid mistakes.

WISDOM 6:9

A blind leper
heard about Braille and asked to learn it.
One of his dreams was to read the Bible.
But the leper made a tragic discovery.
His disease had made his fingers
too insensitive to feel
the raised letters of Braille.
It was a crushing blow.
He was on the verge of total depression.
Then the leper realized
that there was one part of his body
that was still sensitive enough
to be able to feel the letters.
It was his tongue.
And that is how he reads the Bible today.

How eagerly do I read and reflect
on God's word that I may know
"how to act wisely and avoid mistakes"?

Radio is like the Old Testament;
you hear God's Word.
TV is like the New Testament;
you not only hear God's Word
but also see it come alive in Jesus.

Inspired by FULTON SHEEN

THURSDAY
Ordinary Time
Week 32

The spirit of Wisdom . . .
reveals itself in many ways. . . .
Wisdom is more beautiful than the sun. . . .
Evil never overcomes Wisdom.

WISDOM 7:22, 29-30

An old poem describes a man
lying under an oak tree
in the midst of a field of pumpkins.
His eyes went from the big pumpkins
on the plant's tiny vines
to the tiny acorns
on the tree's big branches.
He thought to himself, "God blundered!
He should have switched things
and put pumpkins on tree branches
and acorns on the pumpkin vines."
Then he fell asleep, quite pleased
with the wisdom of his observation.
A few minutes later he awoke abruptly
as an acorn bounced off his nose.
The man massaged his nose and thought,
"Maybe God's way was wiser after all!"

What is one thing I've wondered about
concerning God's wisdom in the handling
of our world? Why might God be right?

For what seems to be God's foolishness
is wiser than human wisdom.

1 CORINTHIANS 1:25

FRIDAY
Ordinary Time
Week 32 _____

*People look at the good things around them
and still fail to see the living God.*

WISDOM 13:1

Gene Perret, a scriptwriter for Bob Hope,
was half listening to a flight attendant
give the usual safety instructions.
Suddenly his ears perked as she said,
"There may be fifty ways to leave
your lover, but there are only five ways
to leave this aircraft."
Moments later she added,
"Please return your seat to an upright
and most uncomfortable position.
Later you may lean back and break
the knees of the passenger behind you."
Reported by DYAN MACHAN

Why can some people look at things
and find humor in them, while others can't?
Why can some people look at things
and find God in them, while others can't?

[If someone]
without a sense of smell declared
that this yellow rose I hold had no scent,
we should know that he was wrong.
The defect is in him, not in the flower.
It is the same way
with a person who says there is no God.
    GARRY O'CONNOR quoting RALPH RICHARDSON

*[The Red Sea parted and the Israelites
were able to "pass over" from slavery
to freedom as God's own people.]
They pranced about like horses . . . ;
they skipped about like lambs
and praised you, Lord, for saving them.*

WISDOM 19:9

Karl Barth compared reading the Bible
to looking out the window of a building
and seeing people down on the sidewalk
gazing at something on the roof.
Of course, you can't see what it is.
You can only make guesses based on
the expression on people's faces.
Israel's crossing of the Red Sea
is a good illustration of Barth's point.
Something marvelous happened.
We may not understand fully what it was,
but, whatever it was, it changed Israel.
And, Israel, in turn, would go on
to change the course of human history.

How prayerfully, reverently,
and imaginatively do I read the Bible,
asking the Spirit's guidance?

*What you bring away from the Bible
depends to some extent
on what you carry to it.*

OLIVER WENDELL HOLMES

SUNDAY
Ordinary Time
Week 33

*[Pointing to the Temple,
Jesus shocked his disciples, saying,]
"The time will come when not a single stone
here will be left in its place;
every one will be thrown down."*

LUKE 21:6

The movie *It Happened Tomorrow*
opens with a businessman wishing
he could buy tomorrow's paper today.
Then an old man appears
with tomorrow's newspaper, saying,
"I've decided to grant your wish."
The rest of the movie deals with
what happens to the businessman
as a result of his "future" knowledge.
Jesus does this in today's reading.
He lets his disciples glimpse the future.
The Church uses this reading
on this next-to-the-last Sunday
of the liturgical year
to invite us to reflect upon the end
of the world—or the end of our life,
whatever comes first.

How prepared am I for the end?

*He basked beneath the sun;
He lived a life of going-to-be,
And died with nothing done.*

AUTHOR UNKNOWN

[The Syrian king, Antiochus Epiphanes,
began persecuting the Jewish people.]
Many . . . preferred to die
rather than break the holy covenant . . .
and many did die.

1 MACCABEES 1:62 63

Antiochus ruled the vassal state of Israel
some 170 years before Jesus' birth.
He was a Greek culture buff
who considered himself an incarnation
of Zeus, the father of the Greek gods.
He proudly called himself
Epiphanes ("God manifest").
Jews called him *Epimanes* ("mad man").
In keeping with his love of Greek culture,
he tried to make the Jews into Greeks.
His first step in this direction
was to try to stamp out their religion.
So he launched a massive persecution.
Some Jews defected,
but many other Jews resisted valiantly.

Have I ever given up—or been tempted
to give up—the *practice* of my faith? Why?

A reporter asked Mother Teresa,
"What's wrong with the Church today?"
Mother Teresa responded, "You and I, Sir.
We are what's wrong with the Church,
for we are the Church."

TUESDAY
Ordinary Time
Week 33 —————————————————

[Ninety-year-old Eleazar was a Jew
who was martyred for his faith.]
His courageous death was remembered
as a glorious example, not only by
young people, but by the entire nation.

2 MACCABEES 6:31

A mother prayed for several years
for her two sons to return to church.
One Sunday she looked up and saw them
sitting across the aisle from her.
Later she asked her sons
what brought them back to church.
They said while vacationing in Colorado,
they picked up an old man one Sunday.
It was pouring down cats and dogs,
and he was limping along in the rain.
He told them he was on his way to Mass
three miles from his mountain home.
It was the courageous example
of this old man that brought them back.

How aware am I of the immense power
my example can have on others?
How am I using it?

The worst danger
that confronts the younger generation
is the example
set by the older generation.

E. C. McKENZIE

A Jewish mother and her seven sons
were arrested. . . . Although she saw her
seven sons die . . . she endured it with
great courage, [assuring each son,]
"God will give you back life and breath
again, because you love his laws
more than you love yourself."

2 MACCABEES 7:1, 20, 23

Sister Ann Catherine Ryan is a member
of a faith-sharing group in Bolivia.
One day the group was reflecting
upon Mary, the mother of Jesus.
A young woman said in frustration,
"How can I identify with Mary?
Did Saint Joseph ever beat her up
or insult her?
Did she have to go to work in a factory
at 4 A.M. and work till 8 P.M.
cracking nuts for a meager wage
to support her child?"

How would I answer the young woman?
Why does God let so many good people
suffer at the hands of evil people?

What we suffer at this present time
cannot be compared at all
with the glory
that is going to be revealed to us.

ROMANS 8:18

THURSDAY
Ordinary Time
Week 33

[The king's officials told Mattathias,
a prominent Jewish leader,]
"Do what the king has commanded. . . .
If you do, you and your sons . . .
will be rewarded with silver and gold."
[Mattathias resisted the temptation
to trade an eternal heavenly reward
for a temporary earthly one.]

1 MACCABEES 2:18

Albert Schweitzer gave up earthly fame
to become a doctor to the poor in Africa.
He writes: "One day, in my despair,
I threw myself into a chair . . .
and groaned . . . 'What a blockhead I was
to come out here . . . !'
Thereupon [an associate] said quietly,
'Yes, doctor, here on earth
you are a blockhead, but not in heaven.' "
That remark to Schweitzer
could also have been said to Mattathias:
"Yes, Mattathias, here on earth
you are a blockhead, but not in heaven!"

How do I sustain my courage and hope
when I am depressed and ready to quit?

God, grant me the courage
not to give up what I think is right
even though I think it is hopeless.
ADMIRAL CHESTER NIMITZ

*Judas [Maccabeus] and his brothers said,
"Now that our enemies have been defeated,
let's go to Jerusalem to purify the Temple
[which had been desecrated]
and rededicate it." . . . For eight days
they celebrated the rededication.*

1 MACCABEES 4:36, 56

The rededication of the Temple
gave rise to the feast of Hanukkah.
One Christian writer compared
the Temple, desecrated by Gentiles,
to the soul, desecrated by sin.
The writer also compared
the rededication of the Temple
to the reconciliation of the soul with God,
after having sinned.
As the rededication of the Temple
erased the disgrace
incurred at the hands of the Gentiles,
so the reconciliation of the soul
erased the disgrace
incurred at the hands of sin.

What form does my reconciliation
with God take after I have sinned?

*The LORD says . . .
"You are stained red with sin,
but I will wash you as clean as snow."*

ISAIAH 1:18

398

SATURDAY
Ordinary Time
Week 33

*[In time, King Antiochus IV's fortunes
reversed themselves dramatically.]
He went to bed
in a fit of deep depression. . . .
Waves of despair swept over him,
until he finally realized
that he was going to die.
[And, suddenly, he realized
how stupidly sinful his life had been.]*

1 MACCABEES 6:8-9

At the dawn of the U.S. space program,
mail flooded in from citizens offering
to sacrifice themselves for the cause.
Some letters were from people
trying to make up for misspent lives.
For example, an ex-convict in Texas
explained that he had a high IQ
and wanted to offer himself
as a guinea pig, saying,
"Perhaps in this way I will be able
to truly atone for my mistakes."

What am I doing to atone for my sins?
What more might/should I do?

*Just as you were once determined
to turn away from God,
now turn back and serve him
with ten times more determination.*

BARUCH 4:28

*[A criminal being crucified with Jesus
said,] "Remember me, Jesus,
when you come as King!"
Jesus said to him, "I promise you that
today you will be in Pardise with me."*
                                    LUKE 23:42-43

The book *The Robe,* by Lloyd C. Douglas,
contains this dialogue between
Justus, an early Christian, and
Marcellus, a Roman officer:

Justus: Jesus is alive. . . .
            Sometimes I feel aware of him,
            as if he is close by. . . . You have
            no temptation to cheat . . .
            when for all you know
            Jesus is standing beside you.

Marcellus: I'm afraid I would feel very
            uncomfortable being watched
            by some invisible presence.

Justus: Not if that presence helped . . .
            keep you at your best.

How does the risen, glorified Jesus
help to keep me at my best?

*Jesus is a path to the lost.
He is a loaf to the spiritually hungry.
He is an arm for the weak.
He is a companion to the lonely.
He is a beacon of hope for all.*

MONDAY
Ordinary Time
Week 34 _____

[God] gave Daniel skill
in interpreting visions and dreams.

DANIEL 1:17

Author Don Akchin writes,
"Many ancient peoples believed
that dreams were direct messages
from gods or prophesies of the future."
Something of this idea persists today.
Author John Sanford's thesis
in *Dreams: God's Forgotten Language*
is that God still wants to use dreams
to communicate with us.
Regardless of whether or not
we accept Sanford's thesis,
it is clear that the Bible portrays God
using dreams as a medium of revelation
(MATTHEW 2:13, 27:19; GENESIS 28:12, 40:5).

Can I recall a dream I once had
that still comes to mind
from time to time?
How do I account for its persistence?

I dreamed I was a butterfly
fluttering hither and thither . . .
I awakened! And now I don't know if
I was a man dreaming I was a butterfly
or if I am a butterfly
dreaming I am a man.

Chinese philosopher CHUANG TZU

TUESDAY
Ordinary Time
Week 34

*[King Nebuchadnezzar of Babylonia
had a dream in which he saw a statue
made of four metals. Suddenly, a stone
broke from a cliff and destroyed it.
Daniel said,] "But the stone grew to be
a mountain that covered the whole earth.
[The stone stood for God's kingdom
and the four metals for worldly empires.
God's kingdom] will completely destroy
all those empires and then last forever."*

DANIEL 2:35, 44

The four empires of Babylonia, Media,
Persia, and Greece took turns dominating
the Near East for over 300 years.
The king's dream foretells
that those four empires will be replaced
by a kingdom established by God.
Gospel writers saw the stone to be Jesus.
Thus Luke says, "The stone which the
builders rejected as worthless [the stone
that broke from the cliff, destroyed
the statue, and covered the earth]
turned out to be the most important" (20:17).

How firmly do I believe
that God is at work in the world and
that God's plan can't be frustrated?

If God is for us, who can be against us?

ROMANS 8:31

WEDNESDAY
Ordinary Time
Week 34

*[The king asked Daniel to reveal
the meaning of the strange writing
that appeared on the palace wall, saying,]
"If you . . . tell me what it means,
you will be dressed in robes
of royal purple, wear a gold chain
of honor around your neck, and
be the third in power in the kingdom."
Daniel replied, "Keep your gifts for
yourself or give them to someone else.
I will . . . tell you what it means."*

DANIEL 5:16-17

A high school student had spent days
painting cartoons and quotations
on the walls of a certain classroom.
When he wouldn't take any money
for the job, the teacher asked the boy's
father what gift he might give the boy.
The father replied,
"The best gift that you can give my son
is the honor of having done something
out of love."

How much are my deeds
motivated by love
rather than out of some other motive?

*God doesn't want our deeds;
God wants the love that prompts them.*
SAINT TERESA OF AVILA

At dawn the king . . . hurried to the pit.
When he got there, he called out . . .
"Daniel . . . ! Was the God you serve . . .
able to save you from the lions?"
Daniel answered, ". . . God sent his angel
to shut the mouths of the lions. . . ."
The king was overjoyed and gave orders
for Daniel to be pulled up out of the pit.

DANIEL 6:19-23

King Darius liked Daniel immensely
and gave him a high office.
Court officials grew jealous of Daniel.
Together they conspired to get the king
to outlaw prayer for a period of time.
Then they lay in wait to catch Daniel,
for they knew that he would continue
to pray faithfully to his God.
Darius had no choice but to enforce
the penalty for disobeying the king: death.
The rest of the story we know.

How firmly do I believe
that if I am faithful to God,
God will be faithful to me? Why?

O Lord, help me understand
that you ain't going
to let nothing come my way
that you and me can't handle together.

AUTHOR UNKNOWN

FRIDAY
Ordinary Time
Week 34 _____

[Daniel had a vision in which he saw]
One like a son of man coming,
on the clouds of heaven. . . .
He received . . . an everlasting dominion.

DANIEL 7:13-14 (NAB)

The gospels refer to Jesus
by the title "Son of Man" about 70 times.
One reference comes at Jesus' trial,
when the high priest asks him, " 'Are you
the Messiah, the Son of the Blessed God?'
'I am,' answered Jesus,
'and you will all see the Son of Man . . .
coming with the clouds of heaven!'
The High Priest tore his robes and said,
'We don't need any more witnesses!
You heard his blasphemy' " (MARK 14:61-64).
Another reference concerns the end
of the world. Jesus himself says of it,
"Then the Son of Man will appear,
coming in the clouds with great power"
(MARK 13:26).

How ready am I
for that incredibly awesome hour
when "the Son of Man will appear,
coming in the clouds with great power"?

The world is a bridge;
pass over it, but don't build on it.

Sign on a bridge in the Near East

[Daniel had yet another vision:
a spectacular scene of judgment
portraying] the power and greatness
of all the kingdoms on earth [being] . . .
given to the people of the Supreme God
[the hour of glory for God's faithful].

DANIEL 7:27

A plaque at Plymouth Rock, Massachusetts,
describes the courage of the Pilgrims
who settled there:
"Here, under cover of darkness,
the fast dwindling company
laid their dead, leveling the earth
above them lest the Indians learn
how many were the graves.
History records no nobler venture for
faith and freedom than this Pilgrim band."
The same could be said of every member
of that countless army of believers
who have remained faithful
during the many religious persecutions
that have dyed red the pages of history.

How faithful am I remaining
during the "persecuting" humdrum of life?

The best argument for an immortal life
is the existence of a person
who deserves one.

WILLIAM JAMES

YEAR-CYCLE SCHEDULE

The following table shows which cycle to follow in the upcoming years.

Liturgical Year	Cycle to Follow
1994/95	C
1995/96	A
1996/97	B
1997/98	C
1998/99	A
1999/2000	B
2000/1	C
2001/2	A
2002/3	B
2003/4	C
2004/5	A
2005/6	B
2006/7	C
2007/8	A
2008/9	B
2009/10	C

Weekly Meeting Format

CALL TO PRAYER

> *The leader begins each weekly meeting*
> *by having someone light a candle*
> *and then reading the following prayerfully:*

Jesus said,
"I am the light of the world. . . .
Whoever follows me
will have the light of life
and will never walk in darkness."

JOHN 8:12

Lord Jesus, you also said
that where two or three
come together in your name,
you are there with them.
The light of this candle
symbolizes your presence among us.

And, Lord Jesus,
where you are,
there, too,
are the Father and the Holy Spirit.
So we begin our meeting
in the presence and the name
of the Father,
the Son,
and the Holy Spirit.